Explo...

The Raymond ... *Memorial* *Lectures*
at Stan... *University*

EXPLORATION INTO GOD

JOHN A. T. ROBINSON

Bishop of Woolwich

Stanford University Press
Stanford, California

The Raymond Fred West Memorial Lectures
on Immortality, Human Conduct, and Human Destiny
were established in 1910 by
Mr. and Mrs. Fred West of Seattle
in memory of their son

Stanford University Press
Stanford, California
© 1967 by the Board of Trustees of the
Leland Stanford Junior University
Printed in the United States of America
L.C. 67-26529

Preface

This book is a considerably expanded version of material delivered as the Raymond Fred West Memorial Lectures at Stanford University, California, in May 1966. I am most grateful for the invitation, for the stimulus the lectures provided, and for the hospitality accorded to my wife and myself.

My original intention had been to devote the lectures to the subject of Christology. But it became increasingly clear that before one could develop the theme "God was in Christ" (which I shall be presupposing in all that follows), one must try to explore further the meaning of "God"—for, as Thomas Altizer has said, "Christ cannot appear as God at a time in which God is dead."[1] And to this further exploration I was much encouraged by some disarmingly gracious words from Father F. C. Copleston, S.J., in an article which he called "Probe at Woolwich":

My basic idea is this. By publishing *Honest to God* the bishop won for himself an extremely wide circle of readers. He succeeded in shocking or startling many people into thinking and talking about theological matters. If therefore he could write for his public, in similarly popular style, a book exhibiting more positively and fully the foundations of his Christian vision of reality, he might do a

[1] T. J. J. Altizer and W. Hamilton, *Radical Theology and the Death of God* (Indianapolis, 1966), p. 135.

v

tremendous amount of good. Perhaps this is an impertinent suggestion to make. But it seems to me that the Bishop of Woolwich is faced with an opportunity which rarely comes to anyone in his position.[2]

I am certain that I have not in fact matched that demand. Indeed I am not quite sure what "my public" is. For *Honest to God* itself did not set out to be a popular book. And the lectures that occasioned this book were prepared for university students and so to that extent were framed for an academic audience.[3] But they were not addressed primarily to those with a professional interest in theology. I have therefore tried to combine a "lay" approach with the kind of scientific rigor which an educated public now properly expects in any field of learning.

Nevertheless I fully expect that this work may fall between two stools. For this is not a piece of *haute vulgarisation* in the classical sense of taking what the scholars are saying and communicating it to an intelligent lay public. That presupposes a relatively stable situation in which there is an agreed body of knowledge or discussion to interpret and disseminate. This I do not believe exists at the moment in the area of the doctrine of God. The theologizing and the popularizing have to be done at one and the same time.

To press on from *Honest to God,* for instance, means being both more fundamental and more radical—not that there should be any conflict between the two, for fundamentals and roots are after all but two metaphors for the same thing. It

[2] *The Month,* July 1965, pp. 365f.
[3] I have attempted to write at a much more popular level on this and other themes in a collection of pieces called *But That I Can't Believe!* (London, 1967).

means digging deeper; and this necessarily involves asking many far from superficial questions, to which profound minds over the centuries have given answers which must be taken into the account. Nevertheless, I am convinced that this digging has to be carried on, if I may so put it, on an open site, with the public looking on and being welcomed to join in. This is a relatively new and exposed place for the theologian to do his creative work, though many of the greatest contributions to theology have in fact been from men who did their best thinking on the frontier—from St. Paul, through Origen, Augustine, Aquinas, and Luther, to Paul Tillich in our own day.

Perhaps the analogy with archaeology is an illuminating one. For archaeology is a field in which there is still room for collaboration between professional and amateur, and in which there is a tradition of popular yet scientific writing of a high order. There will always be the place in theology as in archaeology for the fully annotated academic monograph. And of course there will always be the place for genuine mass communication. But what I suspect we are going increasingly to see is the marketplace rather than the library, the secular city rather than the monastery, as the *normal* place where the original work of serious theology is done. And this is liable to satisfy neither the professionals nor the public. But all one can do is to refuse to burke the difficult questions because they are difficult, to supply the references, not for armor-plating (for one must be prepared to operate more like David than Goliath) but for new openings, and above all to try to be humble in a field where the great have been before and at the same time honest to the questions that are genuinely one's own.

Contents

The human heart can go to the lengths of God.
Dark and cold we may be, but this
Is no winter now. The frozen misery
Of centuries breaks, cracks, begins to move;
The thunder is the thunder of the floes,
The thaw, the flood, the upstart Spring.
Thank God our time is now when wrong
Comes up to face us everywhere,
Never to leave us till we take
The longest stride of soul men ever took.
Affairs are now soul size.
The enterprise
Is exploration into God.

Christopher Fry: *A Sleep of Prisoners*

I should like to change the name "seekers" to "explorers" . . .
We do not "seek" the Atlantic, we explore it.

Christian Faith and Practice in the Experience
of the Society of Friends, Excerpt 125.

Prologue: Quest for the Personal

In the lectures which formed the basis of this book I began, as Chapter 1 indicates, with a brief review of how the current debate about God has come to occupy the place and take the shape that it has. This review was concerned with what the research scholar calls "the state of the question," its public history. But there is also for anyone who comes to an issue after a good deal of personal involvement another train of events, an inside history, which may be equally important for interpreting the direction and thrust of the argument. This is not so appropriate for the public platform but may be a necessary preface for the reader.

I have hesitated before starting this book with what amounts to a condensed spiritual and intellectual autobiography, especially as personal histories are bound to appear tedious, if not obtrusive, to many readers. On the other hand, it has become obvious to me in the course of debate that without some understanding of the motivation behind it, what one says, and even more what one writes, is subject, apparently, to constructions and interpretations which one scarcely recognizes. In personal conversation or in the face-to-face dialogue of question and answer I find that much of this misunderstanding drops away or falls into place. That is why I always prefer if I can to respond to questions rather than to lecture or to preach. But this still leaves the much larger audience that one can reach only through the written word. And I realize that one owes it to them to declare one's presuppositions. This is particularly true of the readership of *Honest to God*. Previous to that book it had not been my experience to find that what I had written was greeted by reviewers as confused, contradictory, or merely badly written. I am only too conscious of all these defects. But I do not think that this book was very much worse in these respects than any others of mine. Nor, I fear, will the last refuge of the ecclesiastical critic— that the Bishop was a sick man when he wrote it—really explain its deficiencies: a slipped disc cannot be held responsible for that amount of lapse. To be sure, as I freely acknowledged, it was tentative, it was thinking aloud, it was trying to find words for what was felt on the pulses. Nevertheless, I believe in retrospect that the real failure of communication, where it existed, was much more at the level of presupposition than of proposition. Where there was no failure, where, to use a distinction made by a Norwegian student at a public discussion, people felt what I meant even when they did not understand what I said, it was because they stood where I stood: they shared a common presupposition and felt a common pinch.

The room for misunderstanding was the greater because in *Honest to God* I was *taking for granted* most of what I believed. I was assuming the relatively limited audience for which I had previously written and was pushing out on the circumference rather than filling in the center. There were several areas of Christian doctrine—notably the Resurrection and Eschatology—on which I had already written extensively and so omitted because I had nothing new at the time that I wanted to say. But, above all, I was presupposing a fundamental conviction and commitment to the heart of the Christian faith—summed up in "the grace of our Lord Jesus Christ and the love of God and the fellowship of the Holy Spirit"—which I scarcely thought it necessary to state. This was the thesis from which I started. And even when questioning its expression or exploring its antithesis,[1] my base was not in doubt. Naturally if that was discounted, the whole perspective would look very different. And I could begin to understand, if still not really enter into, the supposition that I was an atheist (or at any rate trying to have it both ways), or wanted to substitute an impersonal pantheism for Biblical personalism, or immanence for transcendence, or acceptability to secular man for the truth of the Gospel. The only answer to such constructions is to fill in the center—or, rather, since this would involve an entire *apologia pro vita mea,* to draw out the leading thread which, as I see it, has been running through, and giving direction to, everything that I have sought to express.

This is, inevitably, to isolate and oversimplify. But I suppose that all my deepest concerns both in thought and in action—and I cannot separate the theological, the pastoral, and the political—find their center in a single, continuing quest. This is to give expression, embodiment, to the overmastering yet elusive conviction of the *Thou* at the heart of everything. It is a quest for the form of the personal as the ultimate reality in life, as the deepest truth about all one's relationships and com-

---

[1] As for instance in the lecture, given to urge *Christians* to take the challenge of atheism seriously, "Can a Truly Contemporary Person *Not* Be an Atheist?," *The New Reformation?* (London, 1965), Appendix I.

3

mitments. How can one give shape to the conviction that the personal is the controlling category for the interpretation of everything, both conceptually and in action? That it is this is one of those basic acts of trust of which it is impossible to say whether it comes from one's Christian commitment or whether Christianity authenticates itself because it provides its definition and vindication. At any rate it is, as near as I can determine, my central concern, that which chiefly decides what rings a bell, what I respond to as meaningful, significant, stimulating.

And I think the phrase "respond to" is the key. What I have in mind is that which makes one say, "Yes, that's true, that's real—for me." There are so many things one could not have thought up or expressed, but when one hears them or sees them one says "Yes." There is the sense that what is most deeply real is there before one: one is simply catching up on it, entering into it. Pascal's remark has always haunted me: "Thou wouldst not be seeking me if thou hadst not found me." Just *why* does this, on the face of it paradoxical, statement strike one as true—as true as, indeed much more profoundly true than, the more obvious fact that "thou wouldst not be seeking me if thou *hadst* found me"? It is one of those things of which one can simply say that it is so, reality is like that: it is prevenient, life is response—and hence responsibility —to something that encounters one, as it seems, with the claim of a *Thou*. This is the mystery that lies at its heart.

The clue to one's life can therefore be traced to those things to which one has responded, which have taken a hold on one or set up reverberations. In the realm of ideas—which, needless to say, is only a small, though decisive, part of life—I find that what has proved formative has been certain books backed

4

by the influence of persons to whom they meant much. I should never wish to underestimate the power of a person introducing a thought or a thinker to another. That is why I am unashamed to bring frequent quotations and references into my writings. Most readers may pass over them or wish that the man would predigest the matter for them in his own words: but for the occasional reader, at the right time, it may be a window opening on new worlds unknown. And one introduction leads to another. Or so it has often been with me.

I remember clearly the first time this happened to me. The first work of theology of which I recall becoming aware, as opposed to books of religious instruction, was Nicolas Berdyaev's *The Destiny of Man*. The school chaplain, a man for whom I had a great regard, had it with him at a religious discussion group because he happened to be reading it at the time. For some reason it caught my attention—was it 'the sweep of the title, the exotic sound of the author's name, the challenge of its obvious difficulty? At any rate its memory simmered, and some two or three years later I chose it for a College prize. The attempt to read it defeated me, and I put it aside. It had come before its time. But later I found it of consuming interest. I got other Berdyaevs. There were many ideas and allusions to further ideas which I did not understand. But I responded. For he was grappling with great issues, from a breadth of background and with a profundity of mind which fascinated me. It was to him that I owe my introduction to such deep, and near-heretical, thinkers as Origen, Meister Eckhart, and Jacob Boehme. I was fortunate to have discovered philosophy in a form that I now realize corresponded closely to my personalist and existentialist concern, even though I was not to read Berdyaev again for many years.

For though he fired me to read the philosophy of religion after I had finished classics, the reading list that then still dominated the Cambridge syllabus had not caught up on anything so recent as Berdyaev, let alone on the then new Oxford school of linguistic analysis (for which I was at the time not sorry). I was set to read John Caird's *Introduction to the Philosophy of Religion* and other products of English Hegelianism, together with a number of pre-1914 Gifford Lectures. The dominant books on the Cambridge scene were F. R. Tennant's two-volume *Philosophical Theology* and John Oman's *The Natural and the Supernatural*. The former had indeed a special lecture course entirely devoted to it by H. C. L. Heywood, subsequently Provost of Southwell; and to it I went in the autumn of 1940 with one other, a friend who was soon to leave for the R.A.F. and tragically to meet his death in the first mass raid over Cologne. This meant that I found myself in a one-to-one relationship with my lecturer; and to it I owe much. But the moment to which I owe most he has probably quite forgotten. It was one in which in passing he showed me Martin Buber's dull-brown paperback *I and Thou*. And again my curiosity was whetted by his remark that I should find it very difficult, that it would be useless for the Tripos, but that it might transform me.

It did. And, no sooner was the examination syllabus behind me and I had the never to be repeated opportunity of research on any subject that I chose, than I opted for this tiny book— and its relation to the vastness of the Christian doctrine of God —for the subject of my Ph.D. thesis. But already there had been two other influences that affected the direction in which I would go. The first was the theme for a University prize—

"Kant's Ethics and the Christian Moral Ideal"—which was closely related to the special subject for my Tripos examination. This made me steep myself in Kant, who remains surely one of the profoundist thinkers ever to have written on what he called "the kingdom of ends"—that whole realm that deals with the freedom, the autonomy, the unconditional integrity of the personal. The other influence was also the set subject of a prize essay, specifically entitled "The Personality of God."

Accompanying this was the discovery of Kierkegaard, who was at that time being translated into English after an interval of nearly a century. Again I remember very clearly what stimulated me to read him. It was a quotation in a sermon—was there ever so long a quotation in a sermon?—by A. D. Lindsay, the then Master of Balliol. He read the whole of the extract from the *Journals* in which Kierkegaard meditates on the infinitely delicate relationship between power and freedom which requires nothing less than omnipotence in God if man is to be free, because only omnipotence has the power so to retract itself as to leave the other completely free.[2] It was a passage that undoubtedly affected my earliest attempt at original theological writing, on the omnipotence of love to accomplish universal salvation, which later found its way into my first published book.[3] But, more importantly, it opened up Kierkegaard to me, with his vital insight into the significance of the concrete individual person and of truth as "subjectivity"

[2] S. Kierkegaard, *Selections from the Journals,* edited by A. Dru (London, 1938), No. 616.

[3] *In the End, God* .... In the newly revised edition to be published in 1968, it appears in chaps. 11 and 12.

7

—though one of the most formative essays I read was Buber's criticism of Kierkegaard for supposing that the *I* of "the Individual" could be understood out of relation to the *Thou*.[4] This was a time too in which the insights of Buber's thinking were beginning to be popularized, largely through J. H. Oldham's *Christian Newsletter* and his book *Real Life Is Meeting*. Closely parallel (though, as far as I know, independent) ideas had been spread through John Macmurray's books. His *Reason and Emotion, The Structure of Religious Experience*, and *Interpreting the Universe* were to influence me most and introduced a valuable threefold distinction between "instrumental," "functional," and "personal" relationships to supplement Buber's twofold division between *I-Thou* and *I-It*. But he was never able to satisfy me, any more than John Wren-Lewis subsequently, that he really did justice to the dimension of transcendence required to make meaningful talk of divine-human encounter as distinct from purely interpersonal relationships.

The Divine-Human Encounter was in fact the translated title of a work by another author who influenced me greatly at the time, Emil Brunner. This has since been republished, with additional material, under its original title, *Truth as Encounter*, which does more justice to its thesis, namely, that the truth as the Christian knows it is always a relationship a person must be "in" if he is to understand it aright, as a subject in response to a *Thou*. It can never, without distortion, be stated objectively or propositionally. This thesis was to be reflected in the title of my Ph.D. dissertation, *Thou Who Art*, which

[4] *Die Frage an den Einzelnen*, subsequently included in *Between Man and Man* (London, 1947), pp. 40–82.

was chosen in conscious contrast to that of one of E. L. Mascall's books published about that time, *He Who Is*.

Brunner's name is also a reminder that the dominant influence of this period in theology was that of the Neo-orthodox school, whose whole emphasis was on the transcendent personal God of the Biblical revelation. This was the context in which my mind was shaped, and I have never had reason to doubt its basic presuppositions. My only concern has been with the way in which what Bonhoeffer called Barth's "positivism of revelation" made the presentation of this school of theology often so irrevelant to the realities of relationship from which human beings actually begin. In its more extreme form its distrust of all philosophy and its almost pathological abhorrence of natural theology seem to me to require a split, if not a sacrifice, of the intellect as intolerable as that demanded by any Biblicist fundamentalism.

I mention the influence of Continental Neo-orthodox theology mainly to make it clear that an impersonal immanentism of a pantheistic kind for which I have been thought to be arguing has never for me been a live option—though I suppose there is a part of all of us to which the philosophies of a Wordsworth or a Matthew Arnold make their appeal. For they, like the religions of the East, draw attention to an aspect of reality for which Biblical personalism must find a place if it is to satisfy the whole man.

But the main line of my thinking was firmly within the tradition represented by my supervisor for the Ph.D., H. H. Farmer. With John Baillie, who was also to be one of my examiners, he more than anyone else in Britain had assimilated the insights of the *I-Thou* philosophy to the Biblical doctrines of God and man. And it was under his guiding that I explored both the history and the implications of this tradition of thought for how one could speak of personality in God. The very phrase "personality in God," rather than talk of God as "a Person," is a reminder of another book that played a decisive part in shaping my mind, C. C. J. Webb's Gifford Lectures of 1918, *God and Personality*. These set in context how remarkably recent is the phrase "the personality of God." It only came into use as the eighteenth century passed into the nineteenth: prior to that, the category of personality was reserved for the "Persons" of the Trinity. Indeed, the clues to our modern understanding of personality all lie in the nineteenth century. The classical writers had no word for it, and Boethius' definition of *persona* which was to dominate, and indeed freeze, discussion for over a thousand years, was formulated in a *Christological* context. A person, he said, is "an individual substance of a rational nature." This definition was to have a baleful effect. Not only did it try to encompass the mystery of personality in terms of subpersonal categories like substance and nature (perhaps this was inevitable, though Augustine had opened the possibilities of much deeper psychological insight); but, above all, it attempted to define personality without any reference to relationships. An individual substance could be thought of as existing in complete isolation, and all that distinguished a person from other substances was certain qualities of rationality not possessed by things or animals.

The effect of this definition was to be seen in the discussion of the personality of God. Not only could God easily be envisaged as existing *per se* and *a se*, but all that need be predicated of him for him to be personal was certain "attributes" of goodness and knowledge, purpose and power, etc. The fact that, like a human person, such a Supreme Being could stand in quite impersonal relations with other persons did not matter. For the deism of the eighteenth and early nineteenth centuries it was sufficient that God could be shown to be the benevolent Architect and master Minder of the universe. That this watchmaker Deity, the individual Substance of a supremely rational Nature, who did nothing in particular (except for occasional acts of special providence and miracle) and did it very well, should be remote and impersonal in his relationships was in no way thought to be incompatible with his Personality. It is hardly surprising that Feuerbach (one of the earliest users, incidentally, of the *I-Thou* terminology) should have been so passionate in wanting to restore to human *relationships* the attributes which, as he saw it, had been projected onto this Being in the heavens and had there become frozen.

The ghost of deism was never finally laid by the emergence of a much warmer theism, represented at its best in the late nineteenth century by Hermann Lotze. Indeed, it haunts theology still. This was because theism, which saw that an intimate personal relationship of love and freedom between God and his creatures was essential if he was to bear any resemblance to "the God of Abraham, Isaac, and Jacob," let alone "the God and Father of our Lord Jesus Christ," nevertheless still worked with the assumption that this relationship was external rather than internal to the definition of personality. It was this assumption that the *I-Thou* philosophy challenged. The *I* of personality is possible at all only as the *I* of the *I-Thou* —or of the *I-It*—relationship.

The heart of all talk about personality is the reality of a certain quality of relatedness, of being encountered and drawn out by the grace and claim of the *Thou*. This is the center point, the existential reality, which has to be given expression. And the need to speak of "God" derives from the awareness that in and through and under every finite *Thou* comes, if we are open to it, the grace and claim of an eternal, unconditional *Thou* who cannot finally be evaded by being turned into an *It*. This was the reality which the language of "the personality of God" was trying to represent.[5] The image of a super-Person, of a celestial Being, with those rational qualities, seemed strangely peripheral and irrelevant. No doubt he had to be "there" as the invisible telephone exchange, as it were, to which all wires led. But of him in himself, apart from the wires of relationship, one could see or know nothing.

Such was the point, as I see it in retrospect, to which I had come at the stage of my doctoral thesis in 1945, which has since lain unread and unpublished. And there I left the theoretical quest for the form of the personal, to give myself first to pastoral relationships with real people and then to the teaching of New Testament theology and to liturgical and political involvement with equally real people. By the time I returned to the doctrine of God some fifteen years later and tried to gather up what in the interval had been collecting under the surface, I suppose I had come, without realizing it, to the same sort of point which Bishop Berkeley reached in his questioning of Locke's philosophy of substance. Was it really essential, in order to assert the fact of being held in this

---

[5] I. T. Ramsey makes the same point by insisting on the centrality of the notion of "reciprocity" in his essay "A Personal God" in F. G. Healey, ed., *Prospect for Theology: Essays in Honour of H. H. Farmer* (Welwyn, Eng., 1967), pp. 52–71.

inescapable personal relationship as the final, interpretative reality of life, to posit this concept of a divine Person behind the scenes? If his being there seemed peripheral and irrelevant, might it not be actually misleading? Might not the image of this super-Person distract from the reality-in-relationship it was seeking to express by turning people's eyes upward or outward to a Being for whose existence the evidence was to say the least doubtful, instead of focusing attention on "the beyond in the midst"?

So *Honest to God* was born. The underlying concern had not changed. It was still to give expression to the form of the personal at the level of the universe as a whole, to the overwhelming conviction of the ultimate reality of the *Thou* at the heart of all things. To say that this was atheistic because it questioned traditional theism's image of a supreme Being was surely absurd. To say that it was propounding an impersonal God because it used the phrase "the ground of being" was hardly less so. To use such language of God is no more to assert an impersonal Deity than to call him "the rock of our salvation" or, with the very ancient Christian hymn, the "strength and stay upholding all creation." Indeed, it employs the same metaphor as "substance"—that which "stands under." It is, of course, nonpersonal terminology, and as such very limited. In fact, I have since found myself using it less and less. But its point was not to say that God *is* a Substance, or a Ground, but that the utterly personal *Thou*-relationship in which God is known is (to use Buber's metaphor) the umbilical cord of man's very existence: his whole being is rooted in it. Of course, this metaphor, like any metaphor if pressed, is equally unsatisfactory. For the umbilical cord has to be cut. Or rather it has to be replaced, in the process of growth, first by a natural tie of physical response and then by a free relationship of moral and spiritual responsibility. Only so can a person become a person.

Equally beside the point was the supposition that I was trying to substitute immanence for transcendence, to replace the God "up there" or "out there" by one "in here." In fact, as I tried to insist,[6] I was concerned not to abolish transcendence (for without transcendence God becomes indistinguishable from the world, and so superfluous) but to find a way of *expressing* transcendence which would not tie God's reality to a supranaturalistic or mythological world-view which, if not actually falsifying, was largely meaningless for twentieth-century man. Nor was I saying that God is merely a function of human interpersonal relationships—that if there were no men to experience him he would not exist. On the contrary, I would want to say of God with the *I-Thou* philosophers, "Through *Thee, I* am": our existence as men is wholly dependent on his utterly gracious, prevenient reality.

Nor, incidentally, did I ever confine the awareness of God to relationships with persons—though I would, of course, agree that it comes to its highest articulation, as the Bible insists, through the neighbor (and ultimately through *the* son of man) rather than through anything subpersonal. But it is a common misunderstanding of Buber that in distinguishing the *I-Thou* from the *I-It* relationship he was differentiating our relationships to persons and to things. In fact, we can have both kinds of relationships to each, and the *Thou* of God is to be met as much through nature as through history.

[6] With particular explicitness on p. 44 (London, 1963).

14

The emphasis on persons that comes out in my writings (though I have sought to balance it in Chapter 5 of this book) reflects the fact that my world has been more that of human beings in society than, say, Teilhard de Chardin's world of rocks and fossils and organisms in the laboratory.

This reference to human beings in society may serve to introduce a final disclaimer that this language of the *Thou* means a focusing on the *individual,* in morals or in anything else. Personality is essentially a corporate, social phenomenon. Indeed, it was because of this emphasis that I was drawn into New Testament study through the insights of St. Paul on "the body" (the nearest equivalent Biblical concept to our "personality"), which stands for man, and for all life, in the solidarities both of sin and of redemption. And in the introduction to my study of that theme I made it clear that my interest in the subject was as much social and political as it was theological.[7] The same concern for the personal only within the structural nexus of a largely depersonalized society runs through the essays in *On Being the Church in the World,* which came out of the time when I was primarily a Biblical theologian. It also underlies my political engagement and explains why I found myself responding instinctively to men like Reinhold Niebuhr and William Temple, to James Burnham's *Managerial Revolution* (another of the seminal books in my history), and more recently to socially oriented theologians like Peter Berger, Gibson Winter, and Harvey Cox.

To round off this account, I should perhaps add something to say what it was that spoke to me in the authors I mainly

[7] *The Body* (London, 1952), pp. 7–8.

15

drew upon in *Honest to God,* who have not come into view so far. They entered during the "tunnel period" in which the stream I am here attempting to trace went underground. But they were tributaries which together built up to produce something of a breakthrough, at any rate for me. Indeed, I am inclined to think after the event that the most original thing about *Honest to God* (which I called the least original book I had written) was precisely the bringing together of three authors who were in fact very different. I have never claimed that they were saying the same thing or that they could be harmonized without injustice. But at least Tillich, Bultmann, and, on Bonhoeffer's behalf, Eberhard Bethge, his correspondent and biographer, were all gracious enough to say that I had interpreted them aright. What I was doing was quite deliberately to isolate aspects of the thinking of each which together, it seemed to me, posed the same question from different angles. Let me say briefly what in each caused me to respond, and what did not.

In Tillich it was the possibility of a third option between supranaturalism and naturalism, theism and atheism. He offered a way of speaking about God without dependence on the increasingly problematic notion of a supreme Being, an almighty Person. Yet his awareness of the reality of God was personal through and through. Particularly in his sermons, he spoke of the *Thou,* as heard by Prophet and Apostle, in grace and demand, in a manner which made his profoundly simple words heavy with spiritual power. And this was independent of the Platonic ontology through which he sought to give expression to his more systematic thought and to which I have never found myself particularly drawn.

In Bultmann I found a way of interpreting, in terms that

were existentially real, ways of speaking about God and Christ that were in danger of becoming meaningless to an age like ours which can no longer regard myth as in any sense an objective description of what the world is like or how it works. He enabled the personalistic language of the God who acts, and of beings from another world intervening in the affairs of this one, to be understood still in terms of genuinely personal relationship, without dependence on an antique cosmology. Yet there were many things in Bultmann to which I had no wish to be committed—his undue historical skepticism (as it seemed to me) as a New Testament critic, his heavy reliance on Heideggerian existentialism, and, at least in his more extreme left-wing followers, a tendency not merely to locate the meaning of God in statements about man but to equate the two.

In the case of Bonhoeffer, there was one of those immediate recognitions, when I first read extracts from his *Letters and Papers from Prison,* that here was an insight of tremendous potency and consequence. This was his detachment of Christian faith from what he called "the religious *a priori*." In all previous ages and societies there has been a way in for "God" through the presupposition that all men everywhere, if the opening could be found, were at some point religious. There was a sector in the life of the tribe, the village, the individual, which could never be closed by human explanation or control, in which the priest or "minister of religion" operated. But suppose that gap in the circle is closed, or is fast being closed? For such appears to be the effect of the modern phenomenon of secularization. Suppose completely secularized man (if there ever is such an animal) is not going to be religious at all—and we appear to be well on the way there already? Does this mean the end of God, or prayer, or the Church? Bonhoeffer was convinced the answer was "No"; and he began to wrestle in his prison cell with the question "How do we speak in a secular way about God?"[8]

This question is fundamental, as I see it, to all contemporary "exploration into God." It does not in the least mean capitulation to secularism—to the "ism" which would interpret everything in terms of the age or *saeculum* that now is, which is only another form of naturalism, excluding all reference to God and the transcendent. But it does mean taking seriously the phenomenon of secularization, the rapidly increasing autonomy of one department of life after another from religious or metaphysical control. Secular man, "come of age," is no longer dependent as he once was—and it is futile, as well as immoral, to try to subject him to a God whose strength depends on man's weakness and ignorance. The Christian gospel is rather that man is responsible—terrifyingly responsible—in freedom to a God whose strength is made perfect in weakness and suffering.

Bonhoeffer was horrified at the idea of "cheap grace," and no one could have been further from selling the Gospel short to "modern man" if this made it palatable to his presuppositions. And this is a charge that I personally find it difficult to take too seriously. To adapt some words of William Temple I have used before: "I am not asking, 'What will secular man swallow?' I am secular man asking what there is to eat." There has been a pastoral passion running through all my concern with the theology of the personal. And, if there is a defect among those who rely on Bonhoeffer to the exclusion,

---

[8] *Letters and Papers from Prison*, p. 153. The references here and elsewhere are to the revised English translation (London, 1967).

say, of Tillich, it is in a curving in upon itself of evangelistic interest and missionary motive.[9]

But the point I am concerned to make here is that what attracted me to the three writers upon whom I chiefly drew in *Honest to God* was that they were all men whose roots were in Biblical personalism and who were prepared to explore its expression in radically changing circumstances without abandoning its presuppositions. Tillich was one who, to quote one of his titles, could never divorce "Biblical religion" from "the search for ultimate reality."[10] Bultmann was a man so steeped in the world of the New Testament as to feel the full force of its distance from our own, and hence the stumbling block to modern man of many things which are no true part of the offense of the Gospel at all. Bonhoeffer was astringently, perhaps too exclusively, Biblical in his thinking. And long before I personally became a Biblical theologian by specialism my dominating interest was in what Pascal distinguished as the living God, "the God of Abraham, Isaac, and Jacob," in contrast to "the God of the philosophers," the still-life deity, as Brunner put it, who only allows himself to be looked at. One of the formative influences at an early stage of my philosophical research was some almost verbatim notes, derived from an Oxford friend, of lectures given by O. C. Quick on the fundamental contrast between the Hebraic thinking about God in terms of will and personality and the Hellenic attempt to define his essence in the categories of being and perfection.[11] I now realize that this contrast was

[9] This comes out rather clearly in Paul van Buren's book, *The Secular Meaning of the Gospel* (London, 1963), pp. 190–92.

[10] *Biblical Religion and the Search for Ultimate Reality.*

[11] I think the nearest any of this material came to publication was in parts of his book *The Gospel of the New World.*

overdrawn. But there was no doubt on which side I found myself.[12]

I would agree with the great New Testament scholar Joachim Jeremias that one of the central and distinctive features of the Christian gospel is the utterly intimate, personal relationship which is summed up in Jesus' word *Abba* (Father or Daddy).[13] It is this relationship at the heart of the universe, at the very core of reality, for which Christian theology has to find expression—in such a way that it *is* made central to everything else that coheres in it. The problem is that so much traditional God-language, so far from making it the most real thing in the world, seems to many of one's contemporaries, and to so much of oneself, to add nothing—and even to detract from the reality it exists to express. This is the problem to which I have tried to address myself afresh in what follows.

[12] My "Hebraic" bias came out very strongly in *In the End, God* ....
[13] *The Central Message of the New Testament* (London, 1965), chap. 1.

CHAPTER ONE

The Displacement Effect of Theism

There are fashions in theology as in everything else. In each decade or so some area comes into the sharp focus of concern and debate. In the nineteen-twenties and early thirties, under the impact of historical criticism and liberal theology, it was the doctrine of the *person of Christ*. The most influential book of popular theology in Britain was T. R. Glover's *The Jesus of History,* and the report, for instance, of the Doctrinal Commission of the Church of England, which sat during the years 1922–38, was much preoccupied with what could be believed in the twentieth century about the life and person of Jesus Christ.[1] In the late thirties and forties, under the menacing cloud of strange and rival ideologies, attention had become focused on the doctrine of *man.* Illuminated in all its greatness and tragedy by Reinhold Niebuhr's Gifford Lectures, *The Nature and Destiny of Man,* it was chosen, almost inevitably, as the theological issue of the Lambeth Conference of 1948. Then, in the early fifties, as men's minds turned amid the anxieties of the nuclear age to the hope of a new world, came a reminder of the central place in the Christian procla-

---

[1] *Doctrine in the Church of England* (London, 1938).

mation of *eschatology*, or the doctrine of the end. "Jesus Christ the hope of the world" was the natural theme of the 1954 Assembly of the World Council of Churches. By the time the Council met again, at New Delhi in 1961, the focus of ferment and renewal was the doctrine of *the Church* itself. The most lasting outcome of that Assembly was its setting up of the Commission on "the missionary structure of the congregation," just as, subsequently, the central Decree of the second Vatican Council was that on the nature of the Church. And now we are agitated, most deeply of all, by a thoroughgoing reappraisal of the doctrine of *God*. Already this has reached the stage of throwing up its own Baedeker: David Jenkins' *Guide to the Debate about God*.[2]

And yet I detect a difference this time. All the previous debates (with the partial exception of that on *man*, which engaged Christians in dialogue with Marxists and scientific humanists) took place within the Church, which alone is usually interested in matters of theology. Now, however, the debate has broken through. Indeed, though it began with questions raised by Christian theologians, they were not questions arising directly from Church circles. In fact in Church circles they were not being asked, which explains both the relief and the resentment when they were. The interest and response has flowed right across the usual lines which bound the circles both of professional theology and of popular religion; and for the first time the debate has been overheard and entered by representatives of the non-Christian world-religions. "God" is news. Hardly a week passes without articles

[2] It is really a guide to the *background* of the debate. It is very lucid and illuminating on the theologians who lie behind it, but hardly touches on many themes of the debate itself, e.g., secularization, supranaturalism, God-language, the "death of God" theology.

22

and interviews in the secular journals and the mass media. As Alasdair MacIntyre has said, "When not only the *Observer* but also the *New Yorker*, and not only the *New Yorker* but also *Playboy*, finds that theology, even theology in so rapid a form as this, is what their readers will be titillated by, this casts an interesting and not wholly expected light on the situation. God may be dead, but he is also and most certainly making the scene."[3]

And yet this very considerable "revival of interest," as it was designated by a leading British newspaper, is a strange thing. It has coincided at any rate in England, though not in England alone, with a dramatic decline in the number of baptisms, confirmations, ordinations, etc. which set in, I should judge, some two years earlier[4] and certainly cannot simply be attributed to the "damage" done by the debate. Interest in these questions by no means indicates acceptance of the Church's answer to them. Indeed, one has the impression that people are interested in them despite rather than because of organized religion. They feel there is "something there," but are convinced it cannot be what the Church appears to offer them. And the interest is nothing transient or superficial. God —or, just as much, the absence of God—exercises a continuing fascination, like a candle to the moth. Even atheists cannot leave the subject alone. And if the whole debate were about nothing I cannot believe that it would have cut so deep. There is a reality here "soul size," which demands the new and wider chartings of which Christopher Fry speaks. The enterprise is one that engages the novelist, the dramatist, the film

[3] In a review of Ved Mehta's *The New Theologian, Encounter*, March 1967.

[4] See my contribution to the symposium "...And What Next...?" *Prism*, September 1965, pp. 9–17.

producer, the artist and the poet, the philosopher and the psychiatrist, as much as the professional theologian. And if the answer is to be in distinctively Christian terms at all, it must be in terms of a Christ who is inclusive rather than exclusive.

Indeed, a major part of the irrelevance of the churches appears to be their very posing of the question of God. As this has traditionally come to be stated, it signally fails to formulate the real issue. Hence the confusion, which the opinion polls reveal. It has been said that "the creed of the English is that there is no God and that it is wise to pray to him from time to time."[5] But ostensibly at any rate the creed of the English is emphatically that there *is* a God (the latest poll[6] gave 84 per cent[7]—the latest American figure being 97 per cent[8]) and that it is wise to pray to him from time to time (43 per cent, incredibly, said "regularly"). But most of their other answers indicate that in terms of that God they are practical atheists. The percentages of "Yes" and "No" could almost as well be reversed.

The polls merely reflect the fact that somehow the traditional question has ceased to be the right one to ask. People say "Yes" because there is something they do not want to be put in the position of denying. Yet the truer answer might

[5] Alasdair MacIntyre, *Encounter,* September 1963; reprinted in J. A. T. Robinson and D. L. Edwards, eds., *The Honest to God Debate* (London, 1963), p. 228.

[6] *Television and Religion: A Report Prepared by Social Surveys (Gallup Poll) Ltd. on Behalf of ABC Television, 1964.*

[7] This includes both belief in "a personal God" and in "some sort of Spirit or Vital Force." But the distinction between these two is itself in serious need of clearing up. Cardinal Heenan, for instance, in a television comment specifically mentioned me in the latter category. Would he also include Teilhard de Chardin?

[8] Lou Harris Survey, 1965.

be "No." Conversely, I who find the reality of God inescapable would doubtless be recorded among the 16 per cent who could not return a straight affirmative. I was reminded recently of the story of the American magazine which sent a telegram to Einstein: "DO YOU BELIEVE IN GOD STOP PREPAID FIFTY WORDS." For I was asked by a secular journal for one half of a double article on "Do We Need a God?"[9] My immediate reaction was to reply on a postcard (since a telegram was not prepaid): "To the question as put like that, No." But since mine was the half expected to provide the answer "Yes," and I proposed to accept the invitation, the editor might well have wondered what was happening.

Just what *is* happening? I tried to put my finger on it, as I see it, in the opening chapters of *Honest to God,* and in particular in that called "The End of Theism?" I should like to take up the argument from there.

No one can easily deny that there is at any rate a crisis in theism, that is, in the traditional case for belief in the existence of a personal God. Until recently the issue was relatively simple. It was summed up in the title of the book by A. E. Taylor (author of the justly praised article on "Theism" in the *Encyclopaedia of Religion and Ethics*)—*Does God Exist?* To that the theist said "Yes," the atheist "No"—and the Christian, of course, was on the side of the theist. The answer might be in doubt, but not the question. Now, however, the situation is more complicated.

This is not because the Christian has any more inclination toward the classic alternatives to theism, deism on the one hand and pantheism on the other. Deism started from the transcendence of God, his otherness from the world, but failed

[9] Since reprinted in *But That I Can't Believe!,* chap. 13.

25

to do justice to his immanence: it produced a remote, artificer Deity standing in a less than truly personal relationship to his creatures. Pantheism, on the contrary, started from the immanence of God, his oneness with the world, and failed to do justice to his transcendence. And again it conceived the universe in subpersonal terms, with human freedom and personal identity absorbed in an all-pervasive Divinity.

The reality that theism sought to safeguard and enshrine is not at issue, nor has it changed—the reality of the God-relationship as utterly personal and utterly central. There are, indeed, plenty of questions about the status of this reality—whether it describes anything outside us or merely our way of looking at the world, whether the word "God" is any longer meaningful or necessary, whether for many indeed the reality itself may not finally have gone dead, and so on. I propose to look at these questions in later chapters. But for the time being I am taking for granted the spiritual reality or dimension of experience for which men have used the name "God" and which Jesus defined for his followers in terms of *"Abba,"* Father. The immediate question is how that intensely personal, experienced reality can be represented and given expression in a view of the universe that truly makes it central.

The task of theology may be seen as a form of map making —trying to represent the mystery of *theos* (the incommunicable spiritual reality) by a *logos* or word-picture which can be used for the purposes of communication. It involves a translation or transposition from one dimension to another. And to make a map it is necessary to employ what the geographer calls a "projection." In physical geography the most familiar of these is Mercator's projection, named after the famous sixteenth-century Flemish geographer, which performs the not inconsiderable task of transferring a spherical earth onto the oblong pages of an atlas (a name he also invented). There are, of course, many alternatives, which depict the earth as two flat circles or hemispheres, as strung-out segments like slices of a lemon, in cloverleaf form, or in other still more peculiar shapes. Each is as artificial as the other. This in theory we recognize. Yet we still need to be convinced that the shortest distance between two points on the real earth is not always a straight line on our maps. And we have got so used to visualizing the relation of the continents according to Mercator's projection that we forget that they are not "really" thus. It is difficult to believe, for instance, that Moscow is not much further from San Francisco than London, whereas in fact the two capitals are virtually equidistant from the Pacific coast. For most practical purposes until recently the projection was adequate—the distortion only seriously affected countries on the edge of beyond like Baffin Land and Greenland. But to plan an early warning radar system, or even airline schedules, on Mercator's projection is clearly asking for trouble.

But to return to the maps constructed by theology. Any *logos* about *theos* must also employ some projection to depict or represent the spiritual reality with which it is dealing. Usually we are no more conscious of it than we are when looking at an atlas. Indeed, there is one that has so dominated the tradition in which most of us have grown up that we almost forget that the map is not a direct transcript of reality itself. It has the same effect as the Authorized or King James Version in making people think it *is* the Bible. To question it is to question God. Yet we must question it and look at it for what it is.

Theism, like deism (but unlike pantheism), employs what, for want of a better name, may be called the supranaturalist projection. I am inclined, in this context, to retain Tillich's usage and use the term "supranatural" rather than "super-natural." Of course both words mean the same. But "the supernatural" is used so loosely to mean the same as "the divine" (when it does not mean "the spooky") that the more unfamiliar word may serve to pull us up and remind us that what is at issue here is not the reality of God as such but a particular way of representing or describing it.[10] This projection represents the reality of God in human experience by the *existence* of *a* God or gods in some realm above or beyond that of everyday relationships. So the question of God comes out in the form "Do you believe in the existence of a personal God?" or quite simply "Does God exist?"

So familiar are we with this form of the question that the transition is barely observed. It is a help therefore to look at its use in a tradition other than our own.

From time immemorial men have projected their religious convictions onto the heavens and there visualized beings who embodied them. This is a process we recognize readily enough in the gods and goddesses of ancient Greece and Rome. No one seriously believes these beings "existed" on top of Olympus or anywhere else. The realities of Greek and Roman religion, however, remain—insights into the deepest things of life from which we can still learn as we can from the art or

---

[10] Apart from its somewhat misleading title, it is a defect of Jenkins' otherwise excellent *Guide to the Debate about God* that he does not sufficiently distinguish at this point. For him "the end of theism" is equivalent to the end of belief in God, whereas I used the phrase to mean that a particular way of representing the personal reality of God has reached the end of its usefulness. Whether it has or not is another matter, and this is why I put a question mark after my chapter title.

philosophy of the same cultures. The projection[11] or description of these insights as beings inhabiting another, separate world of their own is now accepted for what it is, a personification in terms of superhuman entities of the profoundest realities of spiritual experience. We can acknowledge this without questioning the perception of the realities they sought to portray.

Similarly, the conception of God as *a* Being, a Person—like ourselves but supremely above or beyond ourselves—will, I believe, come to be seen as a human projection. (Most people already recognize this in the case of the Devil.) It is a way of making real and vivid to the imagination, by personification, the conviction that reality at its deepest is to be interpreted not simply at the level of its impersonal, mathematical regularities but in categories like love and trust, freedom, responsibility, and purpose. The real question of God is not the *existence* of a Being whom we visualize as embodying these in his Person. It is whether this conviction about the ultimate nature and meaning of things is true.

I would interject, in passing, that I am not here simply advocating the same position as that taken by Feuerbach in the last century. Feuerbach accused religion of filching *human* values and projecting them as attributes onto an imaginary subject in the heavens. He wanted to restore them to man and reduce theology to anthropology. I believe, on the contrary, that the reality encountered as personal rather than

---

[11] There is, I am aware, a blurring of the line here between the geographer's and the psychologist's use of the term "projection." But they have this in common: they both involve the throwing of the experienced reality, as it were, onto a screen. To recognize the mechanism at work is not in any way to imply that God is merely a projection, that there is no divine reality apart from the projection. It is simply to describe the human process by which the reality comes to be represented as a supranatural figure.

impersonal is indeed of God and not simply of man. My sole question is whether this conviction about the nature of the ultimate must necessarily be framed in terms of the existence of a divine Being.

Until now it has not been necessary for practical purposes to make much distinction between the religious reality and the projection by which it is represented. We have been able, for instance, to dismiss the spiritual inadequacy of the Olympian religion on the grounds that its gods did not "exist." But we are being forced to be more discriminating. For it is beginning to look as if we should be preparing if necessary to detach our own faith from this projection. It is possible that we may *not* need *a* God (hence part of my reluctance to answer "Yes" to the editor's question),[12] just as a Devil is not essential to the spiritual life of most Christians today. In fact, the projection may actually diminish the reality rather than express it.

Such a supranatural Person has hitherto been regarded by most of us as an indispensable focus for the imagination. But then, in the West, we have done our thinking and living, if not in a three-decker universe, at any rate in one divided mentally into two realms, a natural and a supernatural. In India and China and the East generally, men have not. And Eastern religions have not, for the most part, felt the need of this projection. To be sure, this is partly because they have seen the spiritual reality in less dynamic and personalistic terms than Judaism, Christianity, and Islam. But that is a separate issue. It does not of itself explain the phenomenon of the absence of

[12] The other part was a refusal to test the truth or falsity of God by whether or not he can be shown to be an object of human *need*. He may be "intellectually superfluous" and "emotionally dispensable" and yet be an inescapable reality. See "Can a Truly Contemporary Person *Not* Be an Atheist?" *The New Reformation?* pp. 106–22.

"a God" at all in early Hinduism, Taoism, and Buddhism, especially when the perception of reality in the last is so close at many points to the Christian. A non-theistic religion seems almost a contradiction in terms to the Western mind; but, equally, the presentation of reality as a personified Being appears to trivialize it for the Oriental. There are indeed fundamental differences between these religions, which I have no desire to minimize, but their failure to share a common projection has added unnecessary misunderstanding to the spiritual dialogue between East and West.

But the attachment of Christianity to the supranaturalist projection is becoming less and less obvious. For many purposes we still find it virtually impossible to conceive of "God" except as a separate, personified Being. And there is nothing wrong with this projection, any more than there is with Mercator's. But I am convinced that to represent the spiritual reality (in its transcendent aspect) as a Being in another realm is to make it unreal and remote for vast numbers of people today. Not only do they take the projection for the reality and demand "evidence" for the existence of such a Being (often as crudely as Khrushchev's astronauts), but, more importantly, it has the effect of rendering God marginal and peripheral. Men cannot recognize the reality of God in the experienced relationship, because the image which should help to make it vivid locates him in an area in which they no longer *live*. This is the real point I was trying to make in *Honest to God* about the placing of God "up there" or "out there." It is not that people literally believe this and that this is somehow bad.[13] It is that these are "dead" areas. God is banished

---

[13] Ultimately, of course, all spatial terms in relation to God are interchangeable. Cf. *The Cloud of Unknowing*: "In these matters height, depth, length, and breadth all mean the same" (chap. 37); "We have got to take

to the edges of life—to the uncanny (about the only remaining significance for most people of "the supernatural"), to what men still cannot understand or control (so-styled "acts of God"), or to what is revealingly called the "after-life." At the end of their tether men may still turn to the One above—to pray to or to blame; but in the ordinary course of affairs he comes in, if at all, only after the vital connections have been made. Life is completed, for some, by the addition of God. Most others wonder why they should include this extra storey. In any case, the effect is a displacement of him as God. He has ceased by definition to be the *ens realissimum*, the most real thing in the world. He is on or off the edge of the map. No wonder that it is scarcely significant whether 84 per cent say they believe in him or 16 per cent. For the question is no longer in any real sense the question of God. The projection has distorted the reality it was there to express.

This is not a process confined to the secularized West. John Taylor, the author of that remarkable book on African religion *The Primal Vision,* says that Christianity and Islam with their supranaturalist projection have merely confirmed for Africans the irrelevance of the Sky-God Creator. "It seems," he writes, "that Africa endorses the conviction which is growing in almost every part of the world that if God has his being in some realm of the spirit, distinct from, and external to, the processes and relationships of the here and now, then that God and that realm are to all intents non-existent."[14] And it is in this sense that men in the Bible say, "There is no

---

particular care with those two words 'in' and 'up' "—i.e. not to be misled into interpreting them literally (chap. 51). However, psychologically, I am convinced that they can powerfully affect how real we feel God to be.

[14] *C.M.S. News-Letter,* April 1965.

God": he is not operative, he does not function, he is not real. And this lies behind, though it does not exhaust, the current proclamation by *Christian* theologians of "the death of God." Drained gradually but irrevocably of reality, he has become a shadow. Other things are more real—and that not simply visible, material things. Other spiritual distinctions—the difference, for instance, within human relationships, between *I-Thou* and *I-It*—mean much more than the difference between the world and God, the natural and the supernatural. Consequently, the Church, which seems to men to be framing the issue in an unreal way and asking men for commitments they do not find meaningful, appears increasingly irrelevant.

In the past the question of God's existence as a Being has been in practice indistinguishable from his reality for human experience. In what has been called the most Greek phrase in the Bible, the author of the Epistle to the Hebrews writes that "whoever would draw near to God must believe that he exists."[15] Today belief in his existence bears very little relationship to his reality, as the opinion polls show. The identification no longer holds, and I believe, with Tillich, that we should give up speaking of "the existence" of God.[16]

---

[15] Hebrews 11.6.
[16] See his *Systematic Theology,* I (Welwyn, Eng., 1953), 227: "The scholastics were right when they asserted that in God there is no difference between essence and existence. But they perverted their insight when in spite of this assertion they spoke of the existence of God and tried to argue in favor of it. Actually they did not mean 'existence.' They meant the reality, the validity, the truth of the idea of God, an idea which did not carry the connotation of some*thing* or some*one* who might or might not exist. Yet this is the way in which the idea of God is understood today in scholarly as well as in popular discussions about the 'existence of God.' It would be a great victory for Christian apologetics if the words 'God' and 'existence' were very definitely separated except in the paradox of God becoming manifest under the conditions of existence, that is, in the Christo-

For it belongs to a way of thinking that is rapidly ceasing to be ours.

In a thumbnail sketch called "Man and Reality—The History of Human Thought"[17] the Dutch philosopher C. A. van Peursen notes three main ways, so far, in which men have sought to represent and communicate what is real. First, there is the period of "myth," in which the inner and outer worlds are not yet understood as separate entities but continuously interpenetrate. It is a world before any division between science and religion or physics and metaphysics. Second, there is the period of "ontology," when the supernatural becomes disentangled from the natural, subject stands over against object, man separates to the city and the divine forces to the heavens. "Gods and ethical values are given a status as ontological beings, eternal substances, or essences." And books are written "on the nature of the gods." "What is a god?" comments Van Peursen; "that is an interesting subject for a book!" Third, there is the period of "functional" thinking. Substances and supernatural entities are eliminated as unreal. Things are what they do or what can be done with them. Van Peursen illustrates the change to functional thinking by comparing the way medieval man viewed the soul with the way modern man thinks of the I.Q. "An I.Q. is nothing in itself; it is not a hidden entity in our heads: it is merely the result of certain tests." In this

---

logical paradox. God does not exist. He is being-itself beyond essence and existence. Therefore, to argue that God exists is to deny him." See also J. Macquarrie, *Principles of Christian Theology* (London, 1967), pp. 108–9, and L. Dewart, *The Future of Belief* (London, 1967), pp. 176–80.

[17] *Student World*, 56 (1963), 13–21; reprinted in J. Bowden and J. Richmond, eds., *A Reader in Contemporary Theology* (London, 1967), pp. 115–26.

new world, he concludes, "the word 'God' can no longer function as a metaphysical entity."

In the ontological period the way to make God real was to give him an essence and existence of his own, *a se* and *per se*. In a functional age it is to show how he "comes in," how he "works"—*in* the processes of nature and history, rather than behind them or between them. It hardly needs saying that this is a way of thinking very congenial to the outlook of the Bible, which describes reality much more readily in terms of verbs than substantives. But the "ontologist" in us dies hard, and we are convinced that God cannot get on (or is it that *we* cannot get on?) unless he has an established substance and existence of his own, somewhere. If we cease to believe this he must become a nonentity. But in fact precisely the opposite is true. Unless we can represent him in functional rather than ontological terms, he will rapidly lose all reality. As a Being he has no future.

The point can be reinforced by further comparison with God's "opposite number," the Devil, where we may see the consequences of this process a stage further on. Of course, there is a genuine difference between the two in reality-status. In the Christian world-view, what is embodied in the person of the Devil is less than ultimate. As Edward Caird, the Scottish philosopher, put it, "What ought to be rests on a deeper 'is' than what ought not to be." Nevertheless, the process of giving expression to the reality, which is all that here concerns us, is the same in both cases.

The Devil represents that element in human experience which Jung speaks of as the dark side or the shadow. It is profoundly and inescapably real. In former times, to personify it had the effect of making it more real and more vivid. To see Satan as a Person gave him objectivity, substance, "power of being." But gradually the Devil has suffered a severe loss of reality, which by now has become almost total. He has turned into a semi-comic figure. Only a minority of educated Christians today believe in the Devil except as a mythological expression for evil. And in order to make people take the reality of the dark side seriously the least effective way is to insist on the existence of the personification. For this has the opposite effect. The way to bring evil home is to demythologize. Or, rather, it is to show the reality in human experience which the myths have been describing. One may then remythologize, as the psychologists do, though without any suggestion that these figures and archetypes "exist" in the psyche or elsewhere. The irony is that by insisting on the ontological status of the Devil churchmen have powerfully contributed to the reality's being dismissed along with the supernatural figure. In an earlier part of this century an entire generation tried to forget or to suppress "the shadow," in theology as well as in politics.

But though many can now see this with regard to the Devil, few are yet ready to recognize it of the reality of God. A recent book, *The Existence of God as Confessed by Faith,* by the German theologian Helmut Gollwitzer, represents the forceful reaction of traditional orthodoxy to the undermining of what he regards as the objective existence of God as a supernatural Person. And most churchmen would regard him as valiant for the Faith. One can understand this, as the abandonment of the traditional projection does indeed seem, to those of us brought up within an ontological worldview, to threaten a serious loss. But if we wish to communicate with men in a functional age, and indeed with our real selves, we must recognize that faith has no more necessary commitment to this phase of human thought than to the mythological one before it. This is *not* to "give in" to secularism, that is to say, to a closed view of the universe seeking to comprehend life without reference to anything transcendental. It is to recognize the purely neutral process of secularization (another way of describing the transition to functional thinking); and, having taken this into account, to start our thinking about God once again from what, within that way of thinking, is most real for men rather than from what is unreal.

Indeed, not to do this is precisely to invite secularism and precipitate a view of life in which the entire dimension of God and the spirit plays no part at all. It is to court repetition of what happened previously when deism reached the end of the line. For from one point of view the mechanistic materialism of the nineteenth century represents the residue of eighteenth-century deism. When the *deus ex machina,* the God of the gaps, became squeezed out of his universe, the machine without God was the result. Because there were no gaps, there could, on this view, no longer be any place for God. A self-sufficient naturalism took over from supranaturalism.

In the same way, in this century, a God who is presented as the enemy of secularization, who depends on ontological existence for his reality, is merely inviting secularism. If he can no longer "work" in functional society, if he can survive only as a meta-physical[18] entity like "the soul," then

---

[18] The word "metaphysical" is a source of such confusion that I have decided to use it here only of reality conceived, as in this ontological way of thinking, as somehow behind or beyond the scene of sensible phenomena.

place will not be left for him and society will go on without him. Secularism is the direct result of clinging to a God edged out: he cannot be born again at the center of the new world-view.

How this *can* happen, how we may find a projection that expresses rather than destroys his reality for us, is a vitally important question, to which I shall be returning in Chapter 4.

But a word in retrospect about what I have said so far. It may appear to have been somewhat academic and destructive. But my concern has been positive—removing that which removes God. So many people have been prevented from recognizing that what most deeply concerned them had anything to do with God, because their inherited map located him in some *terra ignota* they had not explored and had no urge to explore. Time and again this has come through in the letters I have received, such as are excerpted in *The Honest to God Debate*.[19]

But I am under no illusion that merely stripping away what, for some, has become a misleading image will of itself expose the reality. Bringing men to God is much more than a process of demythologizing. No changes on the map,

---

Originally meta-physics was simply the name for what came *after* "the Physics" in Aristotle's works. From this it came to signify that which was beyond or behind the physical, whether this was natural (like the soul) or supernatural (like spirits or angels). Of course, it can be used more widely for what is truly real, for "how things really are." In this sense, I shall go on to argue, God-language has a metaphysical reference. But in the present confusion it seems to me better to reserve the word "metaphysics" for its traditional use. In an age of functional thinking it is likely to create as many difficulties as it solves, at any rate until we are over the period of transition. Later, of course, we may again be able to use it more freely.

[19] In particular I would draw attention to the letter on pp. 59–62.

in the *logos* or language about God, will in themselves deliver the reality. Indeed, it may well be that the very word "God" is so invincibly linked in men's minds with the supranaturalist projection that whatever we say they will *hear* it as speaking of something peripheral. For them it belongs to another world. As Harvey Cox puts it, "It is heard, often with deference and usually with courtesy, as a word referring to the linchpin of the era of Christendom (past) or as the totem of one of the tribal subcultures (irrelevant)."[20] He quotes Kierkegaard's story of the clown who went around the village shouting that the circus was on fire and pleading for help to put it out, but who was hailed with merriment as an ingenious advertisement to attract men to it. And Cox goes on:

The sociological problem of speaking about God is that the roles of the people who try to do so places them immediately in a perceptual context where what they say can be safely ignored. Of course there remain some people who can still understand what theologians mean when they use the word *God* and other religious terms. These include not only "religious" people but also people whose occupations or family histories have given them a visitor's pass, if not a membership card, to the meaning-world in which theologians and preachers live. Such people can often be found in church laymen's organizations. Academically trained people who specialize in the humanities also qualify.[21]

In circles predominantly composed of such people we should not forget how artificially we are isolated from the vast mass of our contemporaries who have no entrée to this meaning-world. "God" for them may be as dead a word as

[20] *The Secular City* (London, 1965), p. 246.
[21] *Ibid.*, p. 247.

"the Devil." For them, "to speak in a secular fashion of God," as Bonhoeffer demanded, may be not to use the term at all. It may, for instance, mean, like Jeremiah,[22] buying a plot of land in an apparently hopeless situation, witnessing to the "beyond" of faith by an act of political courage, going on caring when others give up, testifying to the openness of any human condition to the possibilities of God's future and the power of the new creation. It may involve, like Jesus in the parable of the sheep and the goats, translating, transubstantiating the encounter with God into service of the homeless and the hungry.[23] This, for most ordinary people, is likely to be how metaphysics, transcendence, eschatology "come out" in functional terms. It is only thus that the Word of God, or the word "God," is made flesh.

But this does not, as I see it, excuse us the intellectual task of constructing new maps. Without maps we cannot move far without losing direction. If they are absent or defective, exploration, even into God, will go round in circles. But before returning, as it were, to the drawing board, I propose to look more closely at that which the maps are meant to be reproducing.

[22] Jeremiah 32.6–44.
[23] Matthew 25.31–46; cf. Mark 9.37: "Whoever receives one such child in my name receives me; and whoever receives me, receives not me but him who sent me"; and Jeremiah 22.16: "He judged the cause of the poor and needy.... Is not this to know me?, says the Lord."

CHAPTER TWO

God—Dead or Alive?

In the previous chapter I began from the map which theology constructs in order to represent or depict the reality of God. Any map employs a projection, and my point was that the traditional supranaturalist projection which has been used by theism now has a serious displacement effect. What was intended to locate this utterly personal reality as the central fact of life now succeeds, for so many people, in banishing it to its margin. Personifying the reality of God in human experience as the existence of a supranatural Being, far from strengthening and sustaining the reality, has the effect in this age of evacuating it of power. It has contributed much to the "death of God" in our day by removing him spiritually to an area in which people no longer live with any significant part of their lives.

But so far we have *assumed* the reality we are trying to map: our attention has been on the *logos*, the word-picture, rather than on the *theos*, the spiritual reality. But just what is this reality, and how are we to put our finger on it? It is here that the map-making analogy fails us. In constructing a map at least what we are mapping is a known geographical location, which stays put. London is there and not here, and once we have plotted its latitude and longitude, the problem is simply how to represent this point in relation to other points.

But the reality of God is not a point within the world. One cannot pin it down like that. Indeed, the word "God" is so slippery and the reality so intangible that many today are questioning whether they have reference to anything that can usefully or meaningfully be talked about. What is it that has got displaced, and what is it that we have to try to re-center? To what reality does the word "God" refer?

But before we go further we must stop to face the challenge whether this is any longer the right question. Should we not rather ask to what reality *has* the word "God" referred, or even to what reality *did* it refer? For there are those who would tell us that "God is dead," and that it is futile to seek the dead among the living.

Before accepting his obituary as final, however, it is necessary to discover just what it is that is being asserted by his "death." And the meaning of this assertion is almost as elusive as God himself. As I see it, there are two main positions, within each of which there are differences of degree. The first is primarily concerned with what has happened to the word, the second with what has happened to the reality.

For the first, it is the word "God" that in our generation has died or is dying. It is a word that has ceased to function, or is burdened with such misunderstanding or misleading associations, or is confined to such a limited meaning-world, as to be obsolescent. If we cannot find a new word, then we must get by without it, at any rate for the time being. This is the position adopted by Harvey Cox in the final chapter of *The Secular City*, from which I quoted previously. But in the body of the book he continues to use the word.

A more extreme version of this is represented by Paul van Buren, the author of *The Secular Meaning of the Gospel*. For him the word "God" belongs irretrievably to the past. It has no future as a way of speaking about "how things are." There will still be those who find it natural to go on talking in this fashion in order to give expression to certain convictions and commitments. But increasingly we shall have to find other ways to express that dimension in human existence to which the word "God" has traditionally drawn attention.

For those who take this position it is primarily the word rather than the reality that has gone dead, and both the writers I have mentioned would in fact wish to dissociate themselves from talk of "the death of God."[1]

It is those in the second position who embrace, and indeed glory in, this slogan. For them it is the reality, not simply the word, from which the life has departed. But within this position too there are important differences. In his earlier book *The New Essence of Christianity*, William Hamilton saw ours as a period of the death of God insofar as a whole generation and not merely an individual seems to be suffering from a sort of dark night of the soul. The "death" of God on this view is really an extension of the absence, or silence,

---

[1] See further Harvey Cox, "The Death of God and the Future of Theology" in W. R. Miller, ed., *The New Christianity* (New York, 1967). There he distinguishes his own position from Van Buren's as follows: "It is not that the word ['God'] means nothing to 'modern man'. . . but that it means so many different things to different people that it blurs communication rather than facilitating it" (p. 381).

or eclipse of God. It may not be final. And one must go on waiting in hope—living before God, as Bonhoeffer said, *etsi non daretur,* even if he is not "there" for us.

But Hamilton has since moved beyond this position.[2] There has, he believes, been a real and permanent loss of any genuine sense of transcendence. There is no God-shaped blank in modern man: he is not in search of a soul. Some hearts may be restless till they find their rest in God—but this is not necessarily so, and is increasingly less so. There is no point in waiting for God, for God will never come. Yet this need not mean despair or moral dissolution. It is not true that anything goes. Man must create his own meaning, and for this Christ can still provide the key.

This death of the God-reality, which Hamilton sees fundamentally as a modern phenomenon, though with its origins in the past,[3] Thomas Altizer wishes to locate in the first century and to celebrate as the heart of the Gospel. In his significantly titled book *The Gospel of Christian Atheism,* the good news of Christianity for him is that the transcendent God emptied, evacuated himself totally in Jesus Christ, in whom he quite literally "died." Since then he has been wholly immanent in history, becoming progressively incarnate in the universal body of humanity. Yet ironically in this extreme form, by the *coincidentia oppositorum* to which Altizer is always appealing, it appears that God is not really dead after all. Only a form of God has died. He still goes marching on, no longer as "an existent Being" but as "a dia-

---

[2] T. J. J. Altizer and W. Hamilton, *Radical Theology and the Death of God.*

[3] "The coming and death of Jesus makes God's death possible; the 19th Century makes it real. And today, it is our turn to understand and accept" ("The Death of God," *Playboy,* August 1966, p. 137).

lectical process."[4] "God moves forward in history," says Altizer, "by negating his present and previous modes of Being. ... Nevertheless, it is crucial to maintain that God remains God or the divine process remains itself even while in a state of self-estrangement."[5]

It is important to distinguish all these positions from classical atheism as expounded, say, by Lucretius or Freud. For this the word "God" does not refer, and never has referred, to any reality. The whole thing is an illusion. God cannot "die" because he has never been alive. For Altizer, on the contrary, "the God who became Christ was once manifest and real as Creator and Lord. Otherwise, it is not possible to speak of ... the self-annihilation of God."[6] Indeed, he goes so far as to say that "only the Christian can truly speak of the death of God."[7] For the Jew, who knows nothing of his self-negation in Christ, God is still very much alive.[8]

In assessment, I should have thought that "the death of God" label was an unfortunate one. I can see its shock value. As Hamilton has put it, "It is just not something that conventional religious people or bishops or officials can pick up and use in their own way, saying, 'Why, we've been saying that all along.' ... The phrase is, you might say, nonsoluble in holy water, even when uttered with extreme unction."[9]

[4] *The Gospel of Christian Atheism* (Philadelphia, 1966), p. 89.

[5] *Ibid.*, p. 88. Cf. p. 91: "God is a forward-moving process of kenotic metamorphosis who remains himself even while passing through a movement of absolute self-negation."

[6] *Ibid.*, p. 90.

[7] *Ibid.*, p. 102.

[8] For a Jewish response to the debate, see R. L. Rubenstein, "Death of God Theology and Judaism" in *After Auschwitz: Radical Theology and Contemporary Judaism* (Indianapolis, 1966), pp. 243-64.

[9] *Playboy*, August 1966, p. 84.

But as a phrase I would agree with Van Buren that in any strict sense it is "logically absurd": "That about which theology has spoken doesn't fall into a category in which being dead and alive seem to apply."[10] As Rubenstein says: "It is more precise to assert that *we live in the time of the death of God* than to declare 'God is dead.' "[11] In fact, only Altizer really says that *God* dies, as opposed to men's apprehension of God. And on inspection the God who died turns out for him to be the "infinitely distant, absolutely alien, and wholly other" Being whom Blake inveighed against as Nobodaddy. And, though release from this Being is indeed good news, I cannot think that it was particularly "ingenious" of Blake, as Altizer claims,[12] to sense that "the God of deism and the God of orthodoxy are identical." That is far too simple an equation. Nor in order to "kill" this God does it appear to me necessary to repudiate the entire dimension of transcendence, and with it the whole witness of the Bible as interpreted by the Christian Church. For Altizer, transcendence and immanence have become polarized as violently exclusive alternatives, instead of being held together in creative tension.

But I have no wish to become involved in an extended assessment of a particular group of writers. This has to my mind been done with real sensitivity and fairness by Thomas Ogletree in his book *The "Death of God" Controversy,* and with his judgments I would almost wholly concur. The controversy could easily prove to be transient,[13] and there are

[10] In an interview for *Forum* (Garrett Theological Seminary, Evanston, Illinois), 1965–66, No. 1, p. 13a.

[11] "Death of God Theology and Judaism," p. 246.

[12] *The Gospel of Christian Atheism,* p. 91.

[13] Indeed, Hamilton himself wrote to me expressing this view even before the end of 1966 (the year in which the controversy "broke") in a private

plenty of signs of the inevitable risks concomitant upon doing theology by journalism. The bubble may well collapse upon itself by lack of what it takes to sustain it from within; or it may be swamped by sheer reaction from the theological right. I believe it would be a pity if either of these things happened. For there is a real issue at the heart of this protest which must be worked through.

The "death of God" is no doubt an unhappy slogan—certainly if it is taken as in any sense referring to a metaphysical event. Yet it has had its value in drawing attention to a phenomenon which I believe *is* more than the absence, silence, or eclipse of God. It is registering the fact that for millions today the living God has been replaced, not by atheism in the sense of a positive denial of God, nor by agnosticism in the nineteenth-century sense, but precisely by a dead God. The reality of God has simply gone dead on contemporary man in a way that has never quite happened before. This is not a matter of people being argued out of one conviction into another; nor does it involve the discrediting

---

letter, from which I quote with permission: " 'The death of God' can now be decently retired, I think. Not because it is false or offensive. But because we do not have the conceptual tools at hand to give it clarity. It is a myth, of course (and we probably need fewer, not more of these), a metaphor, a language event. I am increasingly persuaded that the real issue can be stated thus: Of course, the old god, the old theism, has gone. Even the center knows this. What do you do with that fact? Do you point to some newly perceived reality and give it the name of God? Or do you try to face the religious realities we share in today without the name of God, on the grounds that there are rules by which the name of the Christian God is ascribed to something, and not everything may be so named?" As will become clear, that for which I want to retain at any rate the freedom to use the word "God" is, as I see it, the old reality (constantly indeed having to be re-perceived in a new way) which the God of theism now fails to represent or communicate. Cf. the perceptive survey by W. R. Comstock, "Theology after the 'Death of God,' " *Cross Currents*, 56 (1966), 265–305.

of one intellectual position. To those for whom God has not "died" in any existential way there appears to be no particular problem and no case to answer. Indeed, they genuinely wonder why the old language will not do: for them, and for a part of many others (among whom I would willingly include myself), it continues to serve. But for increasing numbers God is simply not available as a live option.

It may be said that availability was never among the attributes of God anyhow. An available God, a God who is there to be used, is no God. And there is an important sense in which the God that died is the God that never was. The end of God as a stopgap for intellectual laziness or emotional immaturity is the end of an idol. There is much in the atheist critique which is entirely salutary. But I am convinced that there is more to the "death of God" phenomenon than this. For the new situation is that for so many the category of "God" is not available even for a non-idolatrous response. Moreover, more is meant by all this than saying that one particular way of thinking about God, *an* image or projection of God, is dead—though this certainly, as we have seen, has been a potent factor in the decay of living faith. It is simply that "God" is a dead word. It does not *do* anything. It does not signify, or add anything, or bring any illumination. It retains a certain reflected light and residual glory. But from having been the sun of the universe it is now more like the moon. It is still around, somewhere in most people's consciousness, but fundamentally as dead matter.

The first thing to recognize is that, like the moon, it is not alone in this class. There are other realities which have suffered the same change—the Devil, the angels, the supernatural generally, heaven and hell. If one wants to speak of the realities to which these words have referred, the best way may be not to use these words at all. And there are other words that are deeply affected by the same process—for instance, "miracle," "sin," "eternity." The realities to which they refer may be as valid as ever, and there are almost certainly no direct replacements for the old words. Nevertheless, these words belong to a universe of discourse in which any living exchange becomes increasingly restricted. They cannot be used without too much explanation: they are burdened with associations which lie heavy on them.

The death of these words is something which is as true for Christians as for non-Christians. Hence the phenomenon of "Christian atheism"—an apparently total contradiction, which would have been unimaginable to a previous age. I believe, indeed, that it *is* a contradiction, and that "atheism" is the wrong word to describe the new situation. Nevertheless, it must, I think, be recognized that there is a genuinely new situation.

For instance, however confusing it may be to an older generation, it probably now means something quite different to say of a student at a seminary or theological college that he does not know whether he could say he believes in God. In a previous age, and indeed till very recently, it would have been a sure sign that he had "lost his faith." Now it is likely to mean that he is not convinced that the word "God" is a definition that brings his Christian commitment to a point or adds anything to it. He would feel exactly the same about the Devil or the supernatural. These are part of a currency which he doubts whether he can still use with his secular friends or indeed with himself. They belong to a Church ghetto-world—identification with which, through, say, ordination, becomes increasingly problematic. And this is not simply for the reasons that have always made men stumble at the empirical Church and which could be dismissed as lack of humility. It is that to identify with this "currency area" is automatically to render questionable one's ability to do business outside it. For outside it—that is in any part of the human city except the old religious sector—to bring in "God" to give backing or definition to one's deepest commitments appears unnatural, meaningless, or positively falsifying.

But it is not merely that the category is not available to describe the reality. It is also that the reality is no longer available in the way that it was. There has undoubtedly been a change of consciousness, though it is very difficult to define. Time was when God or the gods, the saints or the Virgin Mary, according to the religious idiom, came into every event that we should now look at in an entirely secular way. There was an immediate sense, through the pores and surface of everything, of the numinous, of *mana,* of a presence, which induced a ready feeling of dependence and contingency and of man's evanescence in face of the eternal. The power of religion over *homo religiosus* was something that we can only dimly imagine today. The strength and security of the religious sector, the place of the priest in the life of the village, is something whose loss we scarcely realize until we find ourselves in a culture where it is still presupposed. The demise of all this under the impact of secularization is almost certainly irreversible. However God is available for modern man, it will not be as the power-center of a sacral world-view in which life cannot be organized without him.

Thus far Bonhoeffer, who was certainly no "death of God" theologian. Hamilton and others have gone on to question whether *any* sense of transcendence, of God-dimension, will in future mark the consciousness of ordinary men and women. It is partly that some experiences which men have in the past instinctively associated with God—like awe, wonder, mystery, tragedy, the "sacredness" connected with birth, sex, and death—simply no longer carry such a reference. But it is also that some of the experiences which previously pointed men to God are not available in the same way today. Thus Hamilton writes:

The other night I was out in the back yard with one of my children, who had to identify some constellations for his science homework. When I was young and used to stand under the starry sky, I recall being filled with all the things you were supposed to be filled with: awe, a sense of my own smallness, dependence. But my son is a full citizen of the modern world, and said to me, after he had located the required constellations, ";Which are the ones we put up there, Dad?" He was more interested in what he could do up there than in what he could feel down here. He had become a technological man, and this means something religiously. . . . The death of God lives in this kind of world.[14]

It is difficult to judge whether this is simply the first brash effect of the impact of technology, crowding out the poetic, the imaginative, the mystical element from human life. In so far as it is, I have no doubt that there will be, and indeed already is, a full and proper reaction to this starving of the human psyche. But I think we should be foolish to imagine that nothing decisive has happened or that we shall be able to go on appealing to the sense of the transcendent in the same old way. And the Christian is affected by this change of climate like everyone else. The contribution of the "death

[14] *Playboy,* August 1966, p. 138.

of God theologians" is that they have seen this, and, paradoxically, insisted on continuing to call themselves "theologians." For despite what they sometimes say, and even glory in, theirs is *not* the same position as that of the pure humanist and atheist. And in this paradox lies the point at which I should wish to put my question to them.

For I believe that the situation is more complicated than saying simply that, whereas previously we said "Yes" to God, now we say "No" to him. The very lingering of the term "theologian" betrays the recognition that in the old language there is a pointer to something that we cannot simply deny or eliminate. To reduce is, finally, to falsify. Talk about God cannot be translated into talk about man without loss or remainder. And it is not enough to say, with Van Buren, that it is a poetic, imaginative way of talking about man, without which life in the secular city will be sadly impoverished.[15]

There is a sense in which the new crisis is simply driving theology back to what it has always known and witnessed to, namely, that God is "ineffable," that there is literally nothing that can be said about him without falsification—except that something must be said. All language, all definition is impossible: yet it is necessary that something be said, as Augustine put it of the Trinity, *ne taceretur*—lest by silence the reality should appear to be denied and therefore equally falsified. From one point of view, the meaningless monosyllable "God" simply stands for an "*x*," an asterisk over all human language, signifying that which cannot be expressed yet cannot be eliminated. It is what is represented by the *"neti, neti"* of Hindu theology: "Not this! Not this!" Of any-

---

[15] "The God of Imagination" [An unpublished lecture].

thing we know we can only say with confidence that God is not that: yet we have to say it. The same is expressed in the saying of Lao Tzu, "The *tao* that can be spoken is not the eternal *tao*."[16] Yet this is not an atheist or a humanist statement, asserting that there is nothing beyond. Precisely the opposite. There *is* a beyond—beyond *everything* of which we can speak. It is the same with the Buddhist affirmation of reality. It is arrived at by negation: yet it is certainly not atheist in the sense in which that word is used by atheistic humanism of the West. The reverence of aposiopesis, of speechlessness, is anything but reductionist.

Christian theology, alike in the apophatic (or "disclaiming") tradition of the Eastern Church and in Aquinas' refusal to say anything "univocally" of God,[17] as well as in the *via negativa* of the mystics, has been equally strong on this "No, no." And yet in the Christian community of faith it has always been balanced by an insistence that while it is impossible to define God it is always possible to point to him. While the theologian says of God constantly, "Not this, not this," in the sense that God cannot be identified with anything, the Bible as constantly says, "There is God ... there ... there, and supremely THERE—in the face and in the following of Jesus the Christ." Even in Christ, the Christian theologian is careful to say that God is not defined or contained, in the sense that Jesus *is* God or *vice versa*. Nevertheless, the entire fullness of the Godhead was there bodily; he was the Word, the incarnation, of God. God is not for the Christian simply an "*x*" or an asterisk: the unconditional *is* met here, and from here we can recognize him in all else with which he cannot be equated.

---

[16] *Tao Teh Ching*, I.   [17] *Summa Theologiae* Ia. 13.5.

Ogletree points out how Van Buren, Hamilton, and Altizer all replace the centrality of God by the centrality of Christ. Yet, as he says,

Unconditional loyalty simply cannot be given to a particular historical figure unless something unconditional is disclosed in that figure. Yet when we begin to use such language, we are already moving in the direction of formulating a doctrine of God in order to attest the Reality disclosed in and through the person of Jesus.[18]

Or again,

By acknowledging decisive significance in the person of Jesus, we confess that we discern in him that which both transcends and shapes the totality of experience, which is meant by the word "God."[19]

Any talk of the "lordship" of Christ entails, implicitly or explicitly, a doctrine of God. The "death of God" theology has made a real contribution in drawing attention to changes that cannot be ignored or reversed. Nevertheless, I am convinced that God-language, however little it may be able to say compared with what it used to be able to say (or may say again), stands for that which by its very nature cannot finally be reduced or translated without remainder into anything else. It stands guard against every attempt to persuade us that this is a closed universe, that the beyond, the unconditional, the radically other—all that Jesus represented by the kingdom of heaven or eternal life—is not as real as, or more real than, that for which we are always prepared to settle.

I do not see how Christians without this dimension (how-

---

[18] The "Death of God" Controversy (London, 1966), p. 36.
[19] Ibid., p. 59.

ever they express it) can be Christians at all. That is why Bonhoeffer's question remains, I believe, an inescapable one: "How do we speak in a 'secular' way about 'God'?" For we must speak of God. We cannot simply let this reality go by default, without witness. And yet to speak of "God" is so often today to fail to communicate the reality at all: indeed, it communicates a dead rather than a living reality. To speak of God in a secular way may be not to use the word at all. This was something Bonhoeffer himself recognized: "Perhaps we cannot now even 'speak' as we used to."[20] The reality may have to be witnessed to much more indirectly, obliquely, parabolically, brokenly—in action, in suffering, rather than in words.

But this for anyone in the Biblical tradition is nothing new or alarming. For the Bible, while attaching great significance to the "name" of God, testifies to an equal reluctance to use it. Nothing hangs on words. Indeed, the name for God changes several times within the Pentateuchal tradition, and the one that has become "God" for us (*Elohim*) belongs to its latest strand. The Bible should teach us that we may be free in this matter of language.

And this freedom has been characteristic of the best tradition of Christian theology. In his pioneering book, *The Future of Belief: Theism in a World Come of Age,* the Roman Catholic philosopher Leslie Dewart quotes St. Thomas Aquinas' observation that "wise people do not worry about names"; and he goes on:

Precisely as name, God's name matters little. It is not truly a Holy Name, and we may please ourselves whether we retain it or not.

[20] *Letters and Papers from Prison*, p. 153.

It is our own invention, not God's, and what we have invented we may improve upon. All that matters for the development of the Christian faith is whether we stand ready to discard whatever might come between man and God. For we should not believe in God's name, any more than we should believe in faith: we should believe only in God.[21]

To use the famous image of Lao Tzu, it is the hole in the middle that makes the wheel.[22] The word "God" is useful, not because it fills in what is in the middle, but precisely because it witnesses to that which can never be filled in. In itself the word is expendable, it "says" nothing. But *something like it* is an indispensable necessity if we are to refer to the hole at all. Since there is in fact nothing quite like it—no word that can replace it as a direct substitute—I am convinced that we must be able to go on using it, if only as shorthand. And this means that we must try to redeem it.

It is obviously relatively easy to say that the word "God" is so completely identified with, or fossilized in, one particular image (of *a Being*) that it must either mean this or nothing at all. Such an identification will please both traditionalist Christians and atheist humanists, and it will have the advantage of equating the word with what has come to seem, through familiarity, what Descartes called "a clear and distinct idea." It is more difficult to defend the position that the word has no necessary equation with this image, and to continue using it to safeguard a reality which must be pointed to somehow. The reality is, inevitably, less distinct than one particular image of it, whose function is precisely to simplify, to clarify it for the imagination. But I am persuaded that such a

---

[21] P. 213.
[22] *Tao Teh Ching*, 11.

position should be defended. I believe that we cannot responsibly jettison the word "God" (while freely recognizing that many will not find themselves able or wanting to use it) if we are to explore the territory over which it has traditionally stood guard, even if this territory is represented on our maps by nothing more than the enigmatic warning: "Here be mystery."

I return, therefore, to the question raised at the beginning of this chapter. I am convinced that it is still relevant, and indeed indispensable, to ask in the present tense, and not merely in the past, what is the reality in experience to which the language of "God" has reference. The task of radical theology, as Humphrey Palmer has well put it, is not one of reduction but of location.[23] Where are we to "place" God-language? What, for instance, is the reference of such an affirmation as "Jesus is Lord"? Does such a statement (and by implication all God-talk) tell us something about reality, about how things are? Or does it merely tell us something about the commitment of the person who makes it? If we cannot escape God-language, if it cannot simply be translated into language about man or the world, what is its point of reference?

[23] "To Reduce and to Locate": Two B.B.C. broadcasts reprinted in *The Listener*, April 28 and May 5, 1966.

57

CHAPTER THREE

Locating the Reality of God

"From one point of view," we said earlier, "the meaningless monosyllable 'God' simply stands for an 'x,' an asterisk." From this it might well be asked whether the word represents something worth arguing about at all. Has God not become merely a cipher, a wraith, the smile on the face, as Julian Huxley has put it, of a cosmic Cheshire cat?

It is important here to recognize a difference. From the point of view of what the word connotes, I believe this is true. Or, rather, it is even less than the truth. For in itself the word "God" *is* a strictly meaningless monosyllable. Even in St. Thomas Aquinas' day men had trouble with it.[1] For, as he points out, "nouns are either abstract or concrete"—there are common nouns and proper nouns—and "God" seems to fall into neither category. Indeed, the trouble so often in the past is precisely that it has come to connote too much. It has immediately signified and been equated with a particular image or object. This or that is what "God" has *meant,* only too clearly and unequivocally. To that extent the sifting process of linguistic analysis has been one of stripping down an idol.

[1] *Summa Theologiae* Ia. 13.1.

For God cannot be so identified without ceasing to be God. We cannot say that the word "God" means anything, in the ordinary dictionary sense of being the verbal equivalent of. This is why it cannot be replaced or dispensed with. Any ways of speaking about him that are suggested in order to fill the word with content for a particular age or culture are not substitutes for it. None of these can be made into God without becoming idols. And God is what compels us to use the word "idol."

Yet, as St. Thomas recognized, this does not mean that we cannot say anything about God. For while it is true that of none of these—and indeed of nothing—can we say "This is what 'God' *connotes*," of all of them—and indeed potentially of anything—we can say, at some time or for some person, "This is what 'God' *denotes*." One may say, "Here is God," or "This is God," not in the sense that this or that is an exhaustive definition but in the sense that here, existentially, one is compelled to say: "Surely the Lord is in this place."[2] This is one of the classic confessions of those who know that somehow they must speak of God. In any place, at any moment, it may be necessary to acknowledge the *Thou* that addresses one through all things. In that sense God appears to be much more everywhere than nowhere. The ineffable is omnipresent.

Nevertheless, one must still ask, what is this elusive reality that God-language is trying, not to capture (because it knows it cannot), but to point to? Can we locate God, not in the sense of pinning him down here but not there, but in the sense of designating the kind of reality we are talking about?

[2] Genesis 28.16.

59

To what in human experience does such language have reference?

The first, and traditional, answer to this question, as has already been indicated, is that the word "God" describes an objective, metaphysical, self-existent Being. Theological statements are statements about this Being, his existence, attributes, and activities. Propositions such as "God is almighty" or "God made the world" have objective reference to this Person behind the phenomena, inaccessible to direct human experience but deducible from his effects. Thus, to take an extreme example, when theologians debated among themselves—and split the Church east and west—on whether the Holy Ghost proceeded from the Father and the Son or from the Father through the Son, they may or may not have been arguing about words, but they had no doubt as to what these words referred—the eternal generation and procession of the Persons of the Trinity understood as metaphysical entities, existing prior to, beyond, and apart from any finite apprehension of them. But even the simplest believer who says "God loves me" takes the language to have the same reference. "Is there a God or isn't there?" means, as we have seen, "Does such a Being exist?"

It is this universally held reference of the word "God" among all unsophisticated folk (and until recently among the sophisticated) that has been under fire from the linguistic philosophers. Do such metaphysical statements really mean anything? Precisely what are we saying by such a simple proposition as "God loves me"? What could verify it, or what would finally count against it? And as for the generation and procession of the Persons, how do we know that we are not talking about celestial mermaids, divine figments of the human imagination?

If this is the reality—outside and beyond our experience—to which the language of God refers, then I for one am prepared to concede the force of the attack. It does not in the least follow that God is an illusion or that all the people who have spoken like this have been mistaken. It is simply that if this is the reality, then I do not think we can make statements about it that will finally stand scrutiny. Under pressure, theologians have been compelled to recognize that God-statements cannot have this naïve objective metaphysical reference. Previously they have not been under pressure, and they did not need to discriminate with such rigor. I believe it is thoroughly healthy that they have been made to. Perhaps the critical narrows through which we are passing are temporary (there are already signs that they have been drawn too strait), but I cannot believe that the situation will ever be quite the same again—any more than theological language about Adam and Eve can return to the simplicities of the pre-Darwinian age.

Under this pressure those who want to talk about "God" have been forced to ask themselves what then is the reference of the word if not to such supra-sensible metaphysical entities. The conclusion has been drawn that statements of Christian theology describe not "how things are" in any objective sense, but "how things are for...a man who sees a certain piece of history in a certain way": they characterize the particular perspective on life of a man who acknowledges "Jesus as Lord." In other words, the reality they describe is the reality of a man's own conviction, the ultimacy for him of a certain way of viewing life, his fundamental resolve to think or behave in a certain manner. Paul van Buren, who has given sustained and brilliant expression to this position in his book *The Secular Meaning of the Gospel,* takes over Richard Hare's word "blik" to characterize this fundamental perspective or frame of commitment. God-language, says Van Buren, functions as a way of indicating the finality, grounded in the irreducible reality of "I'm I," of this perspective for the person concerned.

A few illustrations will show how he carries this through:

In saying that *God* raised up Jesus, the disciples indicated that what had happened to them was fundamental to their life and thought.[3]

The doctrine of Providence is significant as an assertion of the strength of the grasp that the Christian's perspective has on him. This is the meaning of the Christian's assertion that nothing can separate him from the love of God in Christ.[4]

In other words, it tells us nothing about "things" but much about "him." Similarly, to call a hope "eschatological" is to make no assertion about the final state of man or the world: it is "to say that one would die rather than abandon it. It indicates the unqualified, undebatable aspect of the Christian's historical perspective."[5] Finally, he reverses the traditional statement that "because... the Christian believes in the Incarnation, he is therefore impelled to take this world, men, and history seriously."[6] Instead, he says, the doctrine of the Incarnation *"expresses* the believer's deep concern with history, the world of men, and the world which man investi-

---

[3] P. 133.   [4] P. 178.   [5] Pp. 154–55.   [6] P. 160.

gates; it indicates that his attitude toward men and their activities is related to his attitude toward a particular piece of history."[7] This is based on the premise that what verifies a person's faith (i.e., his attitude of concern) "gives the meaning of his faith"—a criterion which comes out very explicitly in the following: "If love for the neighbor is the test of 'love for God,' then by the verification principle it is the meaning of 'love for God.' " To be fair to Van Buren, he has a theological, as well as a purely linguistic, basis for this equation:

If the Logos, which is God, has really been made flesh, then we have no need to speak about anything other than this "flesh" which dwelt among us. The command to love God first and the command to love the neighbor, when taken together, *can only mean* that we are to love the neighbor on the model of Jesus and in his freedom.[8]

But it is clear that for Van Buren "God" is fast on the way to becoming an unnecessary category. And indeed he would be content to be called an atheist (though he would not think this very significant). In his judgment, the reality to which "God" refers still exists, but the concept is semantically superfluous: the reality can less misleadingly be described without it.

This conclusion does not disturb me, and if I were convinced that Van Buren's analysis of theological language was adequate, I should follow him. At any rate, the reality—of a man's final perspective on life—to which he says the word "God" is a pointer, is one that is open to inspection and argument. I am not so sure about his confidence that what he is saying is the same as what was intended by classical Christian

---

[7] *Ibid.* Italics mine.   [8] P. 183. Italics mine.

theology and Christology. And this links with my doubt as to whether, by swinging over from a completely objective, metaphysical answer to the question of the reality indicated by the word "God" to a completely subjective, experiential one, he has really given a sufficient account of what theological language is trying to describe.

I would share his concern with the "cash value" of God-statements. What is involved in the way of ultimacy of commitment, is, I would agree, an essential element in deciding the meaning of any supposed affirmation about what is finally real. But I am not happy about the *equation* of "test" and "meaning." To ask "What is the 'payoff'?" as the sole question about the truth or meaning of a statement is to adopt a philosophy of "so what?" which seems to me to leave out other perfectly legitimate questions. For a man to say, "Here stand I: I can no other," may indicate how the truth registers for him: it may show that for him this is a God-statement, which "he would die rather than abandon."[9] But to determine everything by the quality of the commitment is to say nothing of what has evoked that commitment. Luther certainly, if he uttered these words, believed himself to be up against something to which his unqualifiable reaction was the *response*. It said something to him of "how things are" and *therefore* of how things must be for him.

Van Buren would of course agree that the Christian "blik" is not subjective in the sense that the Christian chooses or thinks it up for himself: he is under the constraint of what he

---

[9] This suggests, incidentally, how inadequate this is as a *definition* of "eschatological" statements. These surely, if the word is to have any useful or distinctive meaning, are affirmations of what the believer is convinced *will be true*, not his convictions about anything and everything if only he holds them strongly enough.

"sees" in Christ. Following Ian Ramsey, Van Buren speaks of disclosure situations or occasions of discernment. He allows for the objective element of being convicted by, as well as for the subjective element of being convinced of. But, on inspection, the "given" factor always turns out to be the human, historical occasion of belief—"this piece of history" or some similar phrase.[10] What traditionally would have been described as the divine element of unconditionality confronting the believer *through* the history—that which for Van Buren gives the "blik" its finality—is grounded in the "I'm I" of the subject, not in any *Thou* by which the subject is addressed. It is failure to do justice to the givenness or objectivity of this *Thou* which I believe renders his translation of religious statements less than adequate.

Consider, for instance, the following characteristic affirmations of faith:

Speak, Lord, for thy servant heareth
Thus saith the Lord
Abba, Father
It seemed good to the Holy Ghost and to us
Herein is love, not that we loved God but that he first loved us

and, from Brigham Young arriving with the Mormons at Salt Lake City,

This is the place.

What sort of judgment is being made in these statements? Obviously there is a strong existentialist element of personal conviction. The payoff is there, evidenced by the unshakable commitment of prophet, apostle, and leader. But even more obvious is the testimony to being convicted by something to

---

[10] See *ibid.,* pp. 113-14, 140-41, 155, and 197.

which any commitment is but response. It compels the acknowledgment, "This is it. At this point I have struck bedrock reality, in face of which I can but reply 'Here am I; send me.'" Integral to any God-statement, at any rate in the Judaeo-Christian tradition, is the consciousness of being encountered, seized, held by a prevenient reality, undeniable in its objectivity, which seeks one out in grace and demand and under the constraint of which a man finds himself judged and accepted for what he truly is. In traditional categories, while the reality is immanent, in that it speaks to him from within his own deepest being, it is also transcendent, in that it is not his to command: it comes, as it were, from beyond him with an unconditional claim upon his life. The fact that life is conceived as a relationship of openness, response, obedience to this overmastering reality is what distinguishes the man who is constrained to use the word "God" from the non-believing humanist.

I am not concerned at this moment with whether this relationship is veridical or illusory. I am simply trying to describe the reality to which the Biblical writers and subsequent Christians would testify. It is a relationship in which a man knows himself bound, in which he is not his own, and yet in which alone he knows that his true freedom is to be found. It is this ineluctable relatedness, this being held by something to which one's whole life is *response*, this "answerability" (Brunner), that is the reality, I suggest, to which the language of "God" points. To speak of "God" is to refer neither on the one hand to an existence outside one's experience nor on the other simply to one's own way of looking at the world. It is to acknowledge a relationship, a confrontation at the heart of one's very constitution as a human being, of which one is compelled to say, in existential terms, "This is it. This is the *ens realissimum,* that which is ultimately and inescapably true."

God-statements are statements about the reality of this relationship. Of what lies outside it or beyond it we can say nothing meaningful. Hence the reticence of the Bible even to utter the name of God, as though one were presuming to fill in the hole at the center of the wheel. One can only describe the spokes of relationship, the reality which is God-for-us. One can speak only, as Schleiermacher put it, of "the whence" of my life, of my creatureliness rather than of the Creator in himself.[11] That is why, as Jeremias points out in his book *The Parables of Jesus,* the action of God is so often described, as it were, from our end, in the passive tense: "Knock and *it shall be opened* unto you." That is the side of the door we can see.

The question of God is not a question of describing or defining what or who exists on the other side of the door, outside the relationship. It is the question of whether this relationship is veridical, of whether reality is of such a nature as to "answer" to this sort of knock, not to confound this sort of trust. To affirm belief in God is indeed to assert a faith in "how things are." But it is to make an affirmation not of something beyond our experience or in another world, but of something given in our relationships in this world. It is to say that "deepest down things" (in Gerard Manley Hopkins' phrase)

[11] *The Christian Faith,* 4.4. For a sympathetic interpretation of Schleiermacher's position, see R. R. Niebuhr, *Schleiermacher on Christ and Religion* (London, 1965), pp. 181–96. Cf. Herbert Braun: "God is the whence of my being taken care of and of my being obliged, which comes to me from my fellow men" ("The Problem of New Testament Theology" in J. M. Robinson, ed., *The Bultmann School of Biblical Interpretation: New Directions* [New York, 1965], p. 183).

we can trust the universe not only at the level of certain mathematical regularities but at the level of utterly personal reliability that Jesus indicated by the word "*Abba,* Father!" It is the faith that this is as true and objective a picture of reality as that described by the natural sciences, and more fundamental. The "promise to pay" which it presupposes is not only that of my own commitment. Faith is the trust that what is unconditional for my life, namely (in Christian terms), "the love of God in Christ Jesus our Lord," cannot be conditioned by anything, that nothing in all creation is able to separate from it.

God-statements are statements about the veracity of this relationship. They cannot finally be proved or disproved, any more than human trust or love can finally be proved or disproved. In that sense there is nothing that might occur, as Antony Flew has demanded there should be,[12] which would show conclusively that there is no God. The believer may still say with Job: "Though he slay me, yet will I trust him." Nevertheless, his trust may not be irrational, nor his use of the word "God" meaningless or redundant.

To say of this or that situation, as the Biblical writers do, that "God" is in it is not to start making statements about some supposed metaphysical entity outside it or beyond it; nor is it to say simply "This piece of history is of fundamental importance for my life." It is to say that in and through this event or person there meets me a claim, a mystery, a grace, whose overriding, transcendent, unconditional character can only be expressed by responding, with the prophet, "Thus saith the Lord." Naturally the man who says this may be mistaken (and there were certain tests of the false prophet in

[12] A. G. N. Flew and A. C. MacIntyre, eds., *New Essays in Philosophical Theology* (London, 1965), p. 99.

Israel, though not, of course, final proofs). But it is this dimension of events, this accent of unconditionality attaching
to perfectly ordinary relationships, to which the word "God"
is the pointer and the sign.

It is impossible, once again, to say what the word "God"
connotes (hence the reticence about the "name" or essential
being of Yahveh). It is possible only to say, when one recognizes it, "Yes, this is it again." For, in the words of Van Peursen, "The word 'God' in the Bible has no meaning as such.
But we too often give it a false, supernatural meaning. Then
our interpretation stands between us and the Bible itself. In
the Bible the word 'God' takes on a meaning."[13] As the presence is sensed again and again, men reply: "Surely the Lord
is in this place"; or "God is among you indeed"; or, supremely,
"God was in Christ." Indeed, for the Christian, what he sees
in Christ—not only in the historical Jesus, but in all that led
up to him and in all that has flowed from him—is such as to
make him say: "Yes, this is it, completely. I still cannot say
what 'God' connotes, but I now know what he denotes—as
fully as human flesh and blood can contain it."

Words, images, or descriptions can but try to catch and
express this reality—either, as it were, in terms of "so what" or
in terms of "as if." And both forms of translation fail if offered
as adequate accounts of what God is. The former says, in
effect, that what "God" means is a certain way of life. But
God does not *mean* this. Rather, God-relationships *express*
themselves as this; they "come out" like this in terms of commitment. The latter way of speaking, on the other hand, says
that God *is* a Person and that God-statements describe this
Person. But they do not describe this Person: they describe

[13] "Man and Reality—The History of Human Thought," *Student World*,
56 (1963), 20.

a relationship, of which the nearest human analogy is to be found in the intimacy and the ultimacy of human personal relationship. Traditional theology may often, particularly in popular form, have spoken as though the "as if" could be dropped and its statements directly designated this Being. At its most careful it has not done this. But now it is vitally necessary to be careful—just as in another field it is vitally necessary, in a way that it was not before, to distinguish "history" and "myth."

We live, as Van Buren says, "in an age in which statements about 'how things are' are expected to have some sort of relationship to men's experience of each other and of things."[14] This is a test which I believe theology should welcome. For its statements are not about realities outside our experience of each other and of things. They are statements about our experience of each other and of things in depth, as these relationships are shot through with an unconditional graciousness and demand for which men have found themselves driven to that brief and pregnant word "God." This dimension of reality may be an illusion; but I am not persuaded that, if this is what the word "God" is seeking to designate, it can be dismissed either as meaningless or as superfluous.

I have preferred to speak of the "reality" of God in preference either to the existence or to the experience of God.[15] For "reality" contains within it both the idea of objectivity and that of subjectivity: for what is real must always be real for someone. One can certainly sympathize with Gollwitzer

[14] *The Secular Meaning of the Gospel,* p. 195.
[15] So also S. Ogden, *The Reality of God and Other Essays,* and P. R. Baelz, "Is God Real?" in C. F. D. Moule, ed., *Faith, Fact and Fantasy* (London, 1964), pp. 45–78.

when he warns against the danger he detects in the existential-
ists' reduction of God to a mere function of human existence,
to a determinate of my being.[16] For as such God has ceased
in any meaningful way to be *God*. But such writers as Bultmann and Braun,[17] whom he attacks, are not, as I see it, concerned to deny the genuine awareness of being confronted
by a grace and a demand transcendentally other than myself.
What they are concerned with is the cash value, in empirical
terms, of the "objective" affirmations of traditional Christian
theology.

What *we* can speak of, from our human situation, is the
awareness of being addressed, claimed, and sustained. We can
testify to the relationship, utterly personal in its demand and
succor, in which we know ourselves held. We can say that
however much this awareness seems to come from within,
from the ground of our very being, it confronts us also with
an otherness to which we can only respond as *I* to *Thou*. But
we take the *I-Thou* character of the relationship seriously
when we recognize that of God we can only say *Thou*, not *I*.
Buber speaks of God as "the *Thou* that by its nature cannot
become *It*."[18] But we might say equally that he is the *Thou*
that by its nature cannot become an *I*. We can never put ourselves on the other side of the relationship, as we can with
human beings. Of course we *can*, and do, speak of God both
as "He" and as "I," as though he were another self, a superhuman Person like, but infinitely above, ourselves. But at this
point he has become *a* Being in the subject-object schema.

---

[16] *The Existence of God as Confessed by Faith.*

[17] Braun has answered Gollwitzer in "Gottes Existenz und meine Ges-
chichtlichkeit im Neuen Testament" in the *Festschrift* for Bultmann's
eightieth birthday, *Zeit und Geschichte* (Tübingen, 1964), pp. 399–421.

[18] *I and Thou* (Edinburgh, 1937), p. 75.

Immediately we translate or project the *Thou* of God as another *I*; then we start putting ourselves on the other side of the relationship. We make God finite by encompassing him in our categories of our own selfhood.

The personification of God, inevitable as it may be for creating an image of him (albeit the very thing against which the Second Commandment warns), falls into a further danger, that of the animist or panpsychist, who identifies the *Thou* of every claim upon his life with another "soul." He indeed takes seriously the *I-Thou* quality of *all* relationships—not only those with other human beings but those with nature and with what Buber calls the world of spiritual realities.[19] But he does this by peopling the world with innumerable centers of consciousness like himself—spirits and daemons indwelling everything. The polytheist makes these (or rather a selection of these) into "gods," behind or above the phenomena, each responsible for ordering some aspect of the world. The theist sees a single personal Being at work (with or without subordinate spirits) unifying all experience. Such a personification or hypostatization of the God-reality in any form is a perfectly legitimate projection, an entirely possible "as if," as long as we recognize it for what it is. But it represents a transcript from experience, not the experience itself. All *we* can describe or designate is the grace and claim of the *Thou* from the side of the relationship in which we find ourselves held. In this reserve of utterance the believer is not being subjectivist in the sense of regarding God merely as a function of human existence. On the contrary, he knows that human existence is but a function of this utterly gracious,

---

[19] *"Die geistigen Wesenheiten,"* somewhat misleadingly rendered in the English translation "intelligible forms" (*ibid.*, p. 6).

disturbing, all-encompassing reality to which his life is the response—or this reality cannot properly be given the name of "God" at all.

To conclude, therefore, God-language does not describe a Thing-in-Itself or even a Person-in-Himself. And yet it does more than register our commitments. It points to an ultimate relatedness in the very structure of our being from which we cannot get away. It is a way of keeping guard over the irreducible, ineffable mystery at the heart of all experience. Traditionally, theology—our map of this mystery—has depicted God at the frontier of human existence. But this has come to mean for most people today something at the periphery of their experience or beyond it. Can we work toward a projection that re-centers this reality—not at the boundaries of life where human powers fail but, as Bonhoeffer demanded, at its center and strength, as "the beyond *in the midst*"?

CHAPTER FOUR

An Exercise in Re-centering

In the previous chapter I sought to identify the reality for which men have found themselves constrained to use the name "God" and to determine what is meant by calling this reality "personal." It is not because he is conceived as a Being with personal attributes that God is properly described as personal. That is a secondary phenomenon. It is rather because at the deepest level men have experienced reality as encountering them with the sort of graciousness and claim that we recognize at its highest in the love of another human being (though not of course only there). That is why the New Testament says that "God is love." For in pure personal relationship we have the nearest clue to the nature of ultimate reality. "No man has ever seen God"; but "if we love one another, God abides in us .... He who abides in love abides in God."[1] And the corollary is that a man without love, who is closed to the claim of the *Thou,* cannot know God.

If this then is the central reality, how can we represent it as such on our maps? A defect of the supranaturalist projection is that it has never really succeeded in putting God at the center. It has taken various forms according to men's succes-

[1] See I John 4.7–21.

sive cosmologies. In primitive times God was conceived as "above" a flat earth. In the geocentric Ptolemaic universe, reproduced spiritually in Dante, the center of the circle is occupied, not by God, but by the point furthest from God, hell. In the theological version of the Copernican cosmology, the deism and theism of the eighteenth and nineteenth centuries, God is indeed the Supreme Being, the sun of his universe, around whom all revolves. But like the sun he is still "out there" from the point of view of human life. Transcendence continues to be represented as distance from man. Immanent though he may also be, God is very much of a separate Being, standing over against his creation.

Can we find a projection whereby he is represented as the center, radiating out—as "the within of things," rather than as a Being external to them? Is not perhaps the cry of this generation summed up in the famous passage of St. Augustine's *Confessions*: "Late have I loved thee! For behold thou wert within me, and I outside; and I sought thee outside"?[2] If, to revert to our map-making analogy, God is the pole, the point around which all our existence pivots, should we not use a projection that represents this point at the center rather than off the edge of the map, as in Mercator's projection? To be sure, it is primarily a difference of mapping—of theography, if you like, rather than theology, of how you represent God rather than of what you believe about him. But we are learning in our generation what a fresh appreciation of realities this can introduce. Exploration *into* God is only a change of spatial metaphor, but I believe it may be an illuminating and suggestive one.

How then shall we begin on this venture into the interior? There are, I believe, two tracks in contemporary theology

[2] 10.27.

which promise advance. But at first sight they lead in opposite directions. Leslie Paul has put the matter like this, and I cannot better his summary:

Two considerable theories of history clamor for the loyalty of Christians just now: they are Teilhard de Chardin's evolutionary theories on the one side, and a kind of Christian positivism on the other. De Chardin sees the whole cosmos as in the grip of a great expansive force rolling all things, including men, on towards some cosmic appointment with God. It is Bergson baptized, evolution sacralized. The other, very new Christian-wise, is the opposite doctrine of *secularization,* that men are in charge and rolling away from God. It is associated with such notions as "man's coming of age" and "religionless Christianity." The elements of this doctrine are familiar: man in the modern world becomes more self-reliant and responsible: he looks to his own resources and not to God's: his ways of thinking are pragmatic and functional and exclude the dimensions of the religious and metaphysical. If Christianity is to speak in that world it must demythologize itself and strip itself of metaphysics too.[8]

The contrast is unmistakable, and I have no wish to make out that the two are saying the same thing. Nevertheless I would urge that we should not be compelled to an either-or. Improbable as it may seem, I believe there is a creative tension in a both-and. It is the same combination which I attempted in *Honest to God* between ideas derived from Tillich and those derived from Bonhoeffer. Apparently the two men could not be more different: for the one everything is religious, for the other nothing is religious; the one focuses on ultimate concern, the other on what he called the penultimate questions; the one is a systematizer, the other an anti-systematizer—and so one could go on dividing them into separate

[8] In a review of Harvey Cox, *The Secular City, Prism,* September 1965, p. 97.

camps, philosophical and theological. They do not indeed seem to have felt much in common themselves. There is only one, rather depreciatory, reference to the early Tillich in Bonhoeffer's *Letters and Papers From Prison*,[4] and I have not noticed any serious response to Bonhoeffer's ideas in Tillich's published work—not even in his latest dialogues with students, *Ultimate Concern*, though he was specifically questioned about him. Moreover, the disciples of each tend to find the other's ideas unsympathetic, particularly the disciples of Bonhoeffer with regard to Tillich. Indeed, I have often been faced with incredulity in theological discussion as to how I could hold the two together. William Hamilton, in a colloquium he chaired for me at Cornell University in 1964, described my capacity to bless and sanction both (with Bultmann thrown in as a third) as a piece of "wizardry." But when this reaction comes up I always recognize the voice of the professional theologian, particularly the Protestant theologian. To laymen the two seem to lie together quite easily. At first my response was to say naïvely that both "rang bells" for me and that I refused to have to choose between them. But I am coming to believe that the holding of them together may, as I suggested earlier, be the distinctive contribution of *Honest to God*. And perhaps this is also the characteristically Anglican contribution to the present theological debate—to refuse the logical either-or and to attempt a creative synthesis.[5]

---

[4] P. 180.

[5] The same spirit is characteristic of the Archbishop of Canterbury's most recent book—A. M. Ramsey, *The Sacred and the Secular*. It is not accidental that it is really impossible to place the Anglican contributors to the debate about God in either camp. These include Werner and Lotte Pelz (*God is No More* and *True Deceivers*), H. A. Williams ("Theology and Self-awareness" in *Soundings*, edited by A. R. Vidler, *The True Wilderness*, and an essay in *The God I Want*, edited by J. Mitchell), and John Wren-Lewis

At any rate I believe it is worth someone pointing out how much there is in *common* between the two most lively approaches to the question of God in our current discussion.

Purely for the purposes of an identification parade, let me simply line up representatives of the two main ways of thinking (without implying that they would by any means agree among themselves).

First, the "secularizers," whose inspiration tends to go back to Bonhoeffer and who, as Leslie Paul said, represent a much more recent phenomenon and are mostly younger men. To begin with, I would cite, from Scotland, Ronald Gregor Smith, whose book *The New Man,* published in 1956, must be recognized as a genuine harbinger, since followed by his *Secular Christianity.* From America come authors whom we have already had considerable occasion to quote: William Hamilton, Paul van Buren, and Harvey Cox.[6] If only to indicate that this is not merely a Protestant procession, one should mention Michael Novak's *Belief and Unbelief* and Charles Davis' *God's Grace in History.* Many others could be added, from Germany[7] and elsewhere. But I would particu-

---

(*God in a Technological Age* and numerous articles). And though Leslie Paul in the review quoted above justifiably sees *The New Reformation?* as putting me with the secularizers, with whom indeed I have the greatest sympathy, I suspect the balance of *Honest to God* and of this book is the other way. I simply do not wish to be forced into what I regard as a false choice.

[6] In his "Afterword" to D. Callahan, ed., *The Secular City Debate* (New York, 1966), pp. 197–203, Cox also proposes a synthesis by bringing together Teilhard de Chardin and the secular atheist Ernst Bloch as the most suggestive "leads" for the future of theology.

[7] Notably, already in 1953, F. Gogarten, *Verhängnis und Hoffnung der Neuzeit;* also G. Ebeling, *Word and Faith* (London, 1965), especially "The Non-religious Interpretation of Biblical Concepts," pp. 98–161, and "Worldly Talk of God," pp. 354–62.

larly like to draw attention to the considerable Dutch contribution, made by such men as A. T. van Leeuwen, C. A. van Peursen, J. C. Hoekendijk, and Albert van den Heuvel.[8] Colin Williams' *Faith in a Secular Age* well summarizes this whole movement of thought.

In the other camp are a much more loosely associated group of thinkers whose spiritual affinity is with the cast of mind associated with Tillich. It would be possible to extend this list widely both backwards into time and well beyond the edge of distinctively Christian theology. Apart from Teilhard de Chardin, one might mention Nicolas Berdyaev, Martin Buber, Charles Hartshorne (with disciples such as John Cobb, Schubert Ogden, and Charles Birch), Carl Jung, Alan Watts, and, most recently, Leslie Dewart.[9] Behind several of these (particularly Buber, Berdyaev, and Watts) lies a long tradition of mystical theology, Jewish, Eastern Orthodox, Catholic, and Protestant, and they all of course have roots in much earlier dogmatic and philosophical theology, eastern and western.

[8] Van Leeuwen, *Christianity in World History*; Van Peursen, "Man and Reality—The History of Human Thought," *Student World*, 56 (1963), 13-21; Hoekendijk, *The Church Inside Out*; Van den Heuvel, *These Rebellious Powers* and *The Humiliation of the Church*.

[9] De Chardin, especially *The Phenomenon of Man, Le Milieu Divin, The Future of Man,* and *Hymn of the Universe*; Berdyaev, especially *Freedom and the Spirit, The Destiny of Man,* and *Spirit and Reality*; Buber, *I and Thou* and *Between Man and Man* (the English translations are by R. Gregor Smith, who thus has a foot in both camps); Hartshorne, *The Divine Relativity: A Social Conception of God* and, with William L. Reese, *Philosophers Speak of God*; Cobb, *A Christian Natural Theology, Based on the Thought of Alfred North Whitehead*; Ogden, *The Reality of God and Other Essays*; Birch, *Nature and God*; Jung, especially *Psychology and Religion: West and East* (Collected Works, Vol. XI); Watts, especially *Behold the Spirit* and *Beyond Theology: The Art of Godmanship*; Dewart, *The Future of Belief: Theism in a World Come of Age* (the subtitle indicates his debt to the Bonhoeffer tradition as well).

Although the two groups are so different, they are both equally suspicious of and suspected by what might be called main-line Western supranaturalism, whether in popular religion or professional theology.

The difference between them is one of starting point. Bonhoeffer once remarked that for the Bible "man lives just as much from 'outwards' to 'inwards' as from 'inwards' to 'outwards.' "[10] And this could stand for the difference of approach of the two groups. The latter begin from the inside out (the more traditional approach for theology), the former, in an age when so many doubt whether there even is an inside, from the outside in. But their points of convergence are, I believe, more significant. These I would list under four heads. Together they seem to me to constitute a base from which a contemporary exploration into God could proceed with some hope.

1. The first point of agreement is that a dualistic model of the universe is out. Whether looked at from the outside or the inside, reality for us is all of a piece. As Van Peursen puts it, "There is no supernatural reality, high and lofty, above us. There is only that reality which concerns us directly and concretely."[11] There is no second storey to the universe, no realm of the divine over and above or behind the processes of nature and history which perforates this world or breaks it by supranatural intervention. The traditional divisions with which theology has worked—body and soul, earth and heaven, this world and the other world, the secular and the sacred, the two natures human and divine, and so forth—are decreasingly viable or useful. They are categories which have ceased to

---

[10] *Letters and Papers From Prison*, p. 192.
[11] "Man and Reality . . . ," p. 16.

speak to the consciousness of modern man, who no longer does his thinking in them. He lives in "one world," in every sense. But it is more appropriate to speak in this connection of non-duality (as the Eastern religions also do) than of monism, a word which Teilhard de Chardin, for instance, would repudiate for all his emphasis on unification and which the secularists would reject in favor of pluralism.

2. The implication of this is not the abolition of the transcendent in pure naturalism: it is an apprehension of the transcendent as given in, with, and under the immanent. "The beyond" is to be found always and only "in the midst," as a function and dimension of it. This is a shot-silk universe, spirit and matter, inside and outside, divine and human, shimmering like aspects of one reality which cannot be separated or divided. As Teilhard de Chardin puts it, "In all things there is a within, coextensive with their without."[12] It is what Tillich is appealing to in speaking of God as the ground of being or the depth of existence, and what he tried to catch in calling his system "ecstatic naturalism."[13] For Dewart, God is not an omnipotent Being overruling nature and history: rather, "in God nature can do *anything*,"[14] and "*with* God . . . all things, all history, is possible to man."[15] This same conviction lies behind the refusal to see any final discontinuity between the

---

[12] *The Phenomenon of Man* (London, 1961), p. 56. I have quoted the translation given in the *pensées* in *Hymn of the Universe* (London, 1965), p. 83.

[13] In C. W. Kegley and R. W. Bretall, eds., *The Theology of Paul Tillich* (New York, 1961), p. 341.

[14] *The Future of Belief*, p. 193.

[15] *Ibid.*, p. 197. Cf. Harvey Cox, following Teilhard de Chardin and Karl Rahner: "Man, seen as the steersman of the cosmos, is the only starting point we have for a viable doctrine of God" (D. Callahan, ed., *The Secular City Debate*, p. 199).

depths of the spirit of man and the spirit of God, which in-spired Harry Williams' *Soundings* essay, "Theology and Self-Awareness," and the religious writings of C. G. Jung,[16] as well as the miscalled "reduction" of theology to anthropology in Bultmann and his school. It is this open frontier between God and man that fascinated mystics like Meister Eckhart, Jacob Boehme, and Angelus Silesius, who made such an appeal to Berdyaev.[17] It is what Buber points to when he sees every finite *Thou* as a "glimpse through" to the eternal *Thou*, and God as met "between" man and man.

But this refusal to separate what God has joined together is the basis also of the holy worldliness and the secular sanc-tity inspired by Bonhoeffer. Gregor Smith, for instance, is struggling to represent transcendence not in terms of some sacred super-history over the head of ordinary history but as "God's historicity"—this world shot through for faith with his unconditionality.[18] Similarly Harvey Cox is concerned to disclose the frontiers of social change as the locus of the Kingdom of God: God is to be found where "the action" is, in and through the obedience of what Gregor Smith calls an "authentic secularity."[19] And this comes out in the very "earthed" and often shocking spirituality of this school both Catholic and Protestant, to which I shall be returning in Chapter 6.

3. The other side of this coin is a strong insistence that we can say *nothing* of God *apart* from these relationships. "We cannot speak of God in himself.... We cannot put any con-tent into the concept of God's being. We can only speak in

[16] See also P. W. Martin, *Experiment in Depth*.

[17] As also to Tillich, who wrote the preface to J. J. Stoudt's study of Boehme, *Sunrise to Eternity*.

[18] *Secular Christianity* (London, 1966), especially pp. 110–24.

[19] *Ibid.*, p. 174.

terms of the ways in which we actually encounter otherness."
So Gregor Smith again, who talks of "falling back into the
trusting silence of negative theology."[20] And he is, of course,
echoing Bonhoeffer's theme: "As to the boundaries, it seems
to me better to be silent."[21] This reticence about what theology
can claim or presume to know is characteristic of the "style,"
as William Hamilton calls it,[22] in which any exploration or
soundings[23] can be done today. This is partly conditioned by
the linguistic rigor with which we have to learn to speak, and
which comes out in the use made by Van Buren and others
of the text "He who has seen me has seen the Father." It is
useless, Van Buren says, to ask with Philip, "Show us the
Father": all *theological* speculation must come to rest in this
man.[24]

But from the opposite point of view there is the same tendency toward an apophatic, or dis-claiming, theology. It is
profoundly characteristic of Berdyaev's whole approach, who
insists that it has "no relation to agnosticism."[25] Tillich refuses to say that any statement about God, except that he is
being-itself, is more than "symbolic"[26]—even the affirmation
that he is love. Teilhard de Chardin says remarkably little
about God: his real theology is of the *milieu divin*. Dewart
sees the future lying with greater silence, greater circum-

---

[20] *Ibid.*, p. 123.

[21] *Letters and Papers From Prison*, p. 155.

[22] *The New Essence of Christianity* (New York, 1961), chap. 1.

[23] See especially the preface to A. R. Vidler, ed., *Soundings* (Cambridge, 1962).

[24] *The Secular Meaning of the Gospel*, pp. 146–48.

[25] *Spirit and Reality* (London, 1939), p. 137 and the whole of chap. 6.

[26] *Systematic Theology*, I, 265. Subsequently he goes so far as to say that the only non-symbolic assertion about God is that "everything we say about God is symbolic" (*Systematic Theology*, II [London, 1957], 10). See J. Macquarrie, *God-Talk* (London, 1967), pp. 50–53.

spection, about any names or images of God. And, of course, this *via negativa,* this way of unknowing, has always been a mark of the mystics, as of Jewish theology, Eastern Orthodox spirituality, and Oriental wisdom: "He who knows does not speak. He who speaks does not know."[27] The recovery of this reticence has led to a humility before the truth which shows itself, finally, in the fourth point of convergence.

4. This is the growing conviction that the old dividing lines are not the real ones, which has led to a reassessment of former antitheses and exclusivisms. In the past there was a clear division between theist and atheist. The issue was belief in the existence of a supreme Being, and to that one either said "Yes" or "No" or remained agnostic. Now there is a much more subtle line between those who believe and those who cannot.[28] The problem is wrestled with by Michael Novak in his book *Belief and Unbelief.* "Many a believer," he writes, "feels out of step with others in his generation. He neither believes with the believers, nor disbelieves with the atheists." Nor is he an agnostic: "it is not fear or hesitation that inhibits him." In this situation "he feels spiritually far closer to men like Albert Camus than to many a bishop and theologian." What Christians and humanists have in common is a shared concern, commitment, intention, and this is frequently more significant than how they articulate or define it. "It appears to be this unity in intentionality," Novak goes on, "that leads believers to 'baptize' non-believers, and non-believers to say that believers, are, underneath it all, non-believers."[29]

27 Lao Tzu, *Tao Teh Ching,* 56.
28 See Dewart, *The Future of Belief,* chap. 2 and pp. 184f.
29 (London, 1966), pp. 19, 20.

This is *not* to make out that there is no difference—there are very real differences—but to draw attention to the fact that to all the writers we are looking at, of both schools, the old demarcations appear falsifying and trivial. In his search for the new essence of Christianity, William Hamilton finds himself drawing indiscriminately on Christian and non-Christian novelists, poets, and dramatists. Tillich speaks of the Spiritual Community, both in its latent and manifest forms, as constituting a unity more significant than the division between "insiders" and "outsiders" to the Church. Bonhoeffer spoke of his greater natural sympathy with the non-religious[30] and insisted that "to be a Christian does not mean to be religious in a particular way ... but to be a man."[31] The mystical tradition notoriously flows over all ecclesiastical frontiers. And one of the notable features of our time—as characteristic of the ideal of "Christian presence"[32] associated with Charles de Foucauld and Bonhoeffer as of the writings of men like Tillich[33] and Alan Watts[34]—has been a new openness to and humility before other world faiths. It has become evident that the supranaturalistic projection has bedevilled dialogue especially with the East. Because Buddhism is non-theistic it does not mean that it is atheistic in the Western sense,[35] and its understanding of Reality must be viewed sympathetically

[30] *Letters and Papers from Prison*, p. 154.

[31] *Ibid.*, p. 198.

[32] See *The Christian Presence* series edited by M. A. C. Warren. For a definition of the concept see also Colin W. Williams, *Faith in a Secular Age* (London, 1966), p. 12.

[33] Especially *Christianity and the Encounter of the World Religions*.

[34] Besides those already mentioned, see, among his many other books, *The Way of Zen*.

[35] See D. T. Suzuki, *Mysticism: Christian and Buddhist*, and G. Appleton, *On the Eightfold Path: Christian Presence amid Buddhism*.

alongside the more dynamic Christian view. Or again, because Hinduism has rejected the personification of God, that does not of itself close the possibility of discussion with Christianity:[36] the question is whether or not Hinduism is finally incompatible with what Teilhard de Chardin calls a personalizing universe.

So much for the common points, despite the diversity of expression and accent. What do they all add up to? Here is a summary of a position taken from a non-Christian which I do not think is too wide of the mark. He speaks of "the metaphysic that recognizes a divine Reality substantial to the world of things and lives and minds; the psychology that finds in the soul something similiar to, or even identical with, divine Reality; the ethic that places man's final end in the knowledge of the immanent and transcendent Ground of all being." That, to be sure, is very much in the idiom of those whose movement is from the inside out rather than from the outside in, as one would expect from Aldous Huxley.[37] And it would need restatement in terms of a more personalist, historical world-view. But is there anything in the *projection* which is basically unchristian?

If one had to find a label to replace that of traditional "theism," I would fall back on one that has a respectable pedigree but has never quite succeeded in establishing itself in orthodox Christian circles—namely, "panentheism." This is defined by *The Oxford Dictionary of the Christian Church*[38] as "the belief that the Being of God includes and penetrates the whole

---

[36] See G. Parrinder, *The Christian Debate: Light from the East,* and R. Panikkar, *The Unknown Christ of Hinduism.*

[37] *The Perennial Philosophy* (London, 1958), p. 1.

[38] F. L. Cross, ed. (1957). It notes that the word was coined by K. C. F. Krause (1781–1832) for his own system. The term was used by Baron F. von Hügel (*Essays and Addresses on the Philosophy of Religion,* I, 162f.;

universe, so that every part of it exists in him, but (as against pantheism) that his Being is more than, and is not exhausted by, the universe." It is the view that God is in everything and everything is in God. In the words of the anonymous author of *The Cloud of Unknowing,* "He is the being of all."[39]

In this way of thinking there is a co-inherence between God and the universe which overcomes the duality without denying the diversity.[40] Often indeed, especially in the mystics, one gets expressions of *identity* between the creature and the Creator, the soul and God, which, if taken as dogmatic generalizations, are clearly heretical. But they are no more than attempts to affirm, at a given focus of time or space, an experience of total identification: "For me, this *is* God and God *is* this"; "Here and now I am one with him and he with me." But there is no transference of divine attributes to the subject, and no denying the difference between the self and God. As the author of *The Cloud of Unknowing* puts it in the same passage, "He is thy being but thou art not his."

Similarly, from the "secular" camp one finds the same identification of God or Christ with the "least of his brethren," which created such a furor, for example, when the *Litany for the Ghetto,* to which I shall be returning in Chapter 6 below, was reported in the public press:

> O God, who hangs on street corners, who
> tastes the grace of cheap wine and the sting
> of the needle,
>
> Help us to touch you....

II, 39) and has been adopted extensively by Hartshorne (see especially *The Divine Relativity* [New Haven, 1964], pp. 88–90, and, with W. L. Reese, *Philosophers Speak of God* [Chicago, 1953], Introduction and Epilogue).

[39] *The Epistle of Privy Counsel,* chap. 1.

[40] See at this point particularly A. Watts, *Behold the Spirit* (New York, 1947), pp. 121–54.

O God, whose name is spick, black-nigger,
bastard, guinea and kike,

Help us to know you.

The heavy-handed way in which orthodox churchmen and theologians laid into this as pantheism showed that they evidently failed to distinguish what the linguists would call the language-game being played. As Berdyaev puts it,

Mystics are always suspected of pantheistic leanings and indeed, when an attempt is made to understand them rationally and to translate their experience into the terms of theology or metaphysics, they certainly come very near to pantheism. Yet, while pantheism is in reality a highly rationalistic doctrine, mysticism uses paradoxical and apparently contradictory expressions, because for the mystics both the identity between the creature and the Creator and the gulf which separates them are equally facts of existence. *Mysticism cannot be expressed either in terms of pantheistic monism or of theistic dualism.*[41]

It is the quest for a third alternative between these two which I believe is being pressed upon us so creatively from such different angles today, secular as well as religious. Nowhere does it come to more sensitive expression than in the worldly mysticism of Teilhard de Chardin. For him God veritably "fills" the universe, as Jeremiah put it,[42] permeating all things from within with the luminosity of his diaphanous presence. And this "diaphany of the Divine at the heart of the universe,"[43] "shining forth from the depths of every event, every element,"[44] is characterized by the utter indissolubility

[41] *Freedom and the Spirit* (London, 1935), p. 242 (italics mine); cf. *Spirit and Reality*, pp. 132–37; also Watts, *Behold the Spirit*, p. 129.

[42] Jeremiah 23.23.

[43] *Le Milieu Divin* (London, 1960), p. 15, n. 1.

[44] "The Mass on the World," *Hymn of the Universe*, p. 28.

of transcendence and immanence on which the panentheist (unlike the pantheist) is concerned to insist. Teilhard speaks of "that which in everything is above everything":[45] it *is* not everything, but it shines through everything, for those with the eyes to see it. In the poet's vivid words:

> The world is charged with the grandeur of God.
> It will flame out, like shining from shook foil;
> It gathers to a greatness, like the ooze of oil
> Crushed.[46]

And yet "the minute particular," as Blake called it, is not swallowed up in the all-embracing whole. Indeed, for the poet or the mystic the very "thusness" (to use the Buddhist term) of the particular takes on an infinite significance. He sees "a world in a grain of sand."[47] It is not, says Alan Watts, "because he is a pantheist, [that] the mystic apprehends all things as one with God. He does not see the reality of God behind the illusion of the creature; he sees God in the very reality, entity and uniqueness of the creature, in its very distinction from God."[48] In a truly personal panentheism there is no absorption of the individual in the Absolute. Even in the intensest moment of identification the distinctions of creature and Creator remain. As Jung put it in the closing words of his *Answer to Job,* "Even the enlightened person ... is never more than his own limited self before the One who dwells

---

[45] *Ibid.,* p. 30.
[46] Gerard Manley Hopkins, "God's Grandeur."
[47] W. Blake, "Auguries of Innocence." Cf. his words:
    Seest thou the little winged fly, smaller than a grain of sand?
    It has a heart like thee, a brain open to heaven and hell,
    Withinside wondrous and expansive: its gates are not clos'd;
    I hope thine are not.
[48] *Behold the Spirit,* p. 148.

within him, whose form has no knowable boundaries, who encompasses him on all sides, fathomless as the abysms of the earth and vast as the sky."[49]

This, of course, is what traditional theism has always sought to represent. There is nothing new or unorthodox about it. The only question is whether the classic projection of theism can for most people today succeed in expressing it. In the *content* of what it is affirming panentheism stands nearer to theism. Part of the difficulty is that the *word* sounds very much nearer to pantheism. But instead of avoiding it for that reason it is worth asking *why* pantheism is suspect from the Christian point of view.[50]

In its familiar forms, whether of Eastern religion or of Western intellectualism, pantheism tends toward an aesthetic, impassive, impersonalistic view of life in which the individual loses his significance. It makes for an unhistorical quietism, without political cutting edge or involvement with the neighbor. And it plays down evil and suffering as partial or illusory. In sum, it depersonalizes and dehistoricizes.

Its *advantage* is that it sees God as the inner truth, depth, and center of all being. And this surely is a more promising

---

[49] *The Collected Works,* XI, 470.

[50] Teilhard de Chardin, indeed, while desiring in the last paragraph of *The Phenomenon of Man* "to put an end once and for all to the fears of 'pantheism'" by insisting that "the universal center of unification ... must be conceived as pre-existing and transcendent," nevertheless boldly seeks to redeem the word: "A very real 'pan-theism' if you like (in the etymological meaning of the word) but an absolutely legitimate pantheism—for if, in the last resort, the reflective centers of the world are effectively no more than 'one with God,' this state is obtained not by identification (God becoming all) but by the differentiating and communicating action of love (God all *in everyone*). And that is essentially orthodox and Christian." For a careful assessment of Teilhard's position in relation to pantheism, see H. de Lubac, *The Religion of Teilhard de Chardin* (London, 1967), chap. 14.

projection than visualizing God and the world as existences with separate centers. Theism rejected the depersonalization of God in deism but retained its projection. Can we reject the depersonalization of God in pantheism but retain its projection? Can we, in fact, depersonify but not depersonalize?

I believe that the attempt must be made. It will involve looking in particular at that whole area of doctrine which deals with the relation between God and the world, and seeing how it "comes out" in the new projection.[51]

But, first, I want to end this chapter by trying to bring panentheism out of the world of abstract theological "isms" into that of real life. For the purpose of trying to "re-center" the idea of God is not one of intellectual satisfaction. It is to undo the displacement effect of traditional theism. If it does not in fact achieve this, and relate God to what *is* most real and central, then the exercise is purely academic. I should like therefore to illustrate what a way of life lived radically from this panentheistic perspective could look like. And for this I go to a novel, by the ex-Communist Rumanian writer Petru Dumitriu, called *Incognito,* which in fact stimulated me to pursue this particular line of exploration into God as much as any of the more purely theological influences to which I have found myself responding.[52]

It illustrates beautifully all the four points of convergence I previously mentioned. Profoundly steeped in Eastern European spirituality, it nevertheless speaks straight to the condi-

[51] James A. Pike alludes to this same massive task in an extended footnote in *What Is This Treasure?* (New York, 1966), pp. 45–47.

[52] In what follows I have reproduced some material from an article in which I first tried to set down its significance for the contemporary theological debate: *New Christian,* October 7, 1965, reprinted in *But That I Can't Believe!,* chap. 14.

tion of Western, Bonhoefferian man. It would be impossible to say whether it should be placed in the "mystical" or in the "secularizing" camp, and it well shows up the falsity of any either-or. It is an account of secular sainthood, and makes no pretensions to be avowedly Christian. It speaks of the God dwelling incognito at the heart of all things, disclosing himself in and through and despite the corruptions and inhumanities of life in our generation.

Its theology is unashamedly panentheistic, though it never uses the term. God is in everything and everything is in God—literally everything material and spiritual, evil as well as good. Yet nothing could be further from the typical world of pantheism described earlier, in which the individual loses his significance in an impassive, unhistorical quietism, without political involvement and without any real entry into the depths of suffering and sin.

Here we are in an intensely personalistic world, in which everything depends upon the utterly individual response of love. Indeed it is this that gives the world its meaning and makes it possible to speak in terms of God at all. I quote from the passage in which this first breaks through:

This was it, the sense and meaning of the universe: it was love. This was where all the turns of my life had been leading me. And now everything was truly simple, revealed with a limpid clarity to my eyes as though in a flash of light *illuminating the world from end to end,* but after which the darkness could never return. Why had I needed to search so long? Why had I expected a teaching that would come from outside myself? Why had I expected the world to justify itself to me, and prove its meaning and purity? It was for me to justify the world by loving and forgiving it, to discover its meaning through love, to purify it through forgiveness.[53]

---

[53] (London, 1964), p. 354.

And yet clearly it was not I imposing my meaning, my love on an alien universe. This love was essentially *response* welling up "from some unknown source that was not me but *thou.*"

What name was I to use? "God," I murmured, "God." How else should I address Him. O Universe? O Heap? O Whole? as "Father" or "Mother"? I might as well call him "Uncle." As "Lord"? I might as well say, "Dear Sir," or "Dear Comrade." How could I say "Lord" to the air I breathed and my own lungs which breathed the air? "My child"? But He contained me, preceded me, created me. "Thou" is His name, to which "God" may be added. For "I" and "me" are no more than a pause between the immensity of the universe which is Him and the very depth of our self, which is also Him.[54]

This illumination of unspeakable meaningfulness at the heart of everything comes in the novel only after nearly three-quarters of it has elapsed, and at the moment of utter dehumanizing degradation and torture.

They went on beating me, but I learnt to pray while the screams issued mechanically from my ill-used body—wordless prayers to a universe that could be a person, a being, a multitude or something utterly strange, who could say? We say "Thou" to it, as though to a man or animal, but this is because of our own imperfection: we may no less say "Thou" to the forest or the sea. We say "Thou" to the universe and hear its voiceless answer in our hearts as though it were a person and had heard us. But it is He who prays within us and answers the prayer which is His gift.[55]

It is the ability to take up *evil* into God and transform it that is the most striking—and shocking—feature of this theology.

[54] *Ibid.,* p. 356.   [55] *Ibid.,* p. 358.

"But you're giving the world the name of God, which is monstrous!" cried Erasmus. I asked if it was monstrous of me to call him Erasmus. I used the name of God because it was a way of directing towards the world all the worship, veneration and prayer which our forebears had devoted to gods growing increasingly less circumscribed; until they became the God of the monotheistic religions, defined by the universe, or by evil, or by His own goodness and perfection, or by reason. Erasmus burst out: "You must be mad! Do you mean that this God of yours is not perfect?" "Yes. He is perfect, but He is also terrible and evil. He is both perfect and imperfect. He is all things, and He confines himself to none."[56]

God is in everything. All things, all events, all persons are the faces, the incognitos of God. This naturally brings protest.

"In fact, you're nothing but an atheist," he said. "You've no real religious feeling at all. To include evil and imperfection in the concept of God is outrageous and immoral." I answered that the idea of a single God had at one time been attacked in similar terms, and that I could not disregard what I had seen with my own eyes in the course of my life.[57]

This refusal to exclude any experience from the raw material of theology is courageous in its honesty if nothing else.

God is everything. He is also composed of volcanoes, cancerous growths and tapeworms. But if you think that justifies you in jumping into the crater of an active volcano, or wallowing in despair and crime and death, or inoculating yourself with a virus —well, go ahead. You're like a fish that asks, "Do you mean to say God isn't only water, He's dry land as well?" To which the answer is, "Yes, my dear fish, He's dry land as well, but if you go climbing on to dry land you'll be sorry."[58]

[56] *Ibid.*, pp. 403–4.   [57] *Ibid.*, p. 405.   [58] *Ibid.*, p. 407.

What is required is not to accept everything as it stands but to "vanquish lethargy" in the seemingly impossible response of love.

What is difficult is to love the world as it is now, while it is doing what it is doing to me, and causing those nearest to me to suffer, and so many others. What is difficult is to bless the material world which contains the Central Committee and the *Securisti*; to love and pardon them. Even to bless them, for they are one of the faces of God, terrifying and sad.[59]

Yet

If I love the world as it is, I am already changing it: a first fragment of the world has been changed, and that is my own heart. Through this first fragment the light of God, His goodness and His love penetrate into the midst of His anger and sorrow and darkness, dispelling them as the smile on a human face dispels the lowered brows and the frowning gaze.[60]

Nothing is outside God. I have sought to love in as far as may be. I have tried to keep within the radiance of God, as far away as possible from His face of terror. We were not created to live in evil, any more than we can live in the incandescence that is at the heart of every star. Every contact with evil is indissolubly linked with its own chastisement, and God suffers. It is for us to ease His sufferings, to increase His joy and enhance His ecstasy. I made friends in the crowd, at meetings, in the sports stadium and coming out of the cinema, as a rule only for a moment, linked with them by a friendly exchange of words, a smile, a look, even a moment of silence. And in closer contacts my discovery spread slowly but constantly from one person to another, in that dense and secret undergrowth which is wholly composed of personal events.[61]

[59] *Ibid.*, p. 458.   [60] *Ibid.*, p. 459.   [61] *Ibid.*, p. 432.

It is this fellowship of the "secret discipline" of love that constitutes the invisible leaven of the kingdom of God. For this, he is saying, no labels are necessary, and any structure kills it.

This is essentially a theology of the latent, rather than of the manifest, Church. And we should listen to it as that, rather than criticize it for what it is not. There is nothing specifically, let alone exclusively, Christian about it. But there is one explicit reference to Christ on which it is fitting to end:

It was in that cell, my legs sticky with filth, that I at last came to understand the divinity of Jesus Christ, the most divine of all men, the one who had most deeply and intensely loved, and who had conceived the parable of the lost sheep; the first of a future mankind wherein a mutation of human hearts will in the end cause the Kingdom of God—the Kingdom, Tao, Agarttha—to descend among men.[62]

Comment would be an anticlimax. But perhaps in the light of this "diaphany of the divine," penetrating the darkness and unintelligibility of things from within, we may see fresh significance in some words of St. Paul's: "The same God who said, '*Out of* darkness let light shine' has caused his light to shine *within* us, to give the light of revelation—the revelation of the glory of God in the *face* of Jesus Christ."[63]

[62] *Ibid.*, p. 383.
[63] II Corinthians 4.6 (N.E.B.). Italics mine.

CHAPTER FIVE

The Divine Field

The scope of this chapter is that vast area of theology which has sought to relate the reality of God to that of the world and which has traditionally included the doctrines of creation, providence, and miracle, of design in nature and purpose in history, together with the problems of evil and suffering. Clearly no attempt can be made in a single chapter, or even in a single book, to cover such a field. All that can or will be done is to show how the change of projection suggested in the last chapter could affect the *approach* and to illustrate from this crucial area of doctrine the kind of difference it could make.

I have not found it easy to find a title for the chapter that would indicate its scope and emphasis. By choosing the one I have I am attempting to signify the fact that for panentheism "the world" is not simply something that can be joined to "God" by the word "and," as in traditional theistic discourse, but that it is in God and God is in it in a way that perhaps enables one to talk of "the divine field" as a physicist might talk of a magnetic field. But all analogies, especially impersonal ones, are very hazardous. I shall come back to this suggestion in the final chapter.

Nowhere more than in this area of theology is the influence

to be felt of what has been called the "long shadow" of deism. The doctrine of creation has been rendered well-nigh incredible for many today by the hangover of what Alan Watts brilliantly caricatures as *deus faber,*[1] the artificer God, the master Potter, Planner, and Producer of the universe. Western tool-making man has allowed himself to become fixated by this mechanistic imagery, when hardly anything could be less appropriate to the processes of evolutionary growth —to what Sir Alister Hardy, the biologist-philosopher, in the title of his Gifford Lectures[2] calls "the living stream." But even where the imagery has been modified (Dorothy Sayers, for instance, proposed substituting that of the author or playwright)[3] the presupposition has remained of *a* Creator, who was there before the world began and who will be there after it has finished, the starter and sustainer of the whole drama. The doctrine of creation has meant that the universe took its origin in, owes its continuance to, and will be brought to consummation by, a Person conceived on the model of a cosmic Supremo.

In the eighteenth century, indeed, this supreme Being was still regarded as necessary in the role of resident engineer. Newton, as Charles Birch reminds us, "was unable to account for the precise orbs of the planets in terms of his mechanics. So he supposed that God personally intervened when they went off their paths. The universe was like a self-winding clock that ran pretty well on the whole, but it could get out of time. Then it was necessary for God to return to regulate it."[4] Equally, for Kant, God was in the last analysis indispensable

---

[1] *Beyond Theology* (London, 1966), pp. 24–25, 62–63.
[2] *The Living Stream* with its sequel *The Divine Flame.*
[3] *The Mind of the Maker.*   [4] *Nature and God* (London, 1965), p. 16.

to the moral system. This system was self-validating, and yet God had to be there to ensure the final coincidence of virtue and happiness which otherwise nothing could guarantee. This was "the God of the gaps," concerning whom the nineteenth century was overwhelmingly to endorse Laplace's famous words to Napoleon: "I have no need of that hypothesis." But the effect was to render God still more of an outsider to the process. He had no place within the system nor right to intervene. The *deus ex machina* led to the *machina sine deo*.

Theism, in contrast, has always insisted upon an intimate, continuous, fatherly relationship between God and every part of his creation. He is indeed transcendent, yet he is also immanent in all his works. Nevertheless, classical theism failed to establish a genuine reciprocal relationship between this Being and the world. This is the point of criticism that is developed by Schubert Ogden,[5] following Hartshorne. For Aquinas, for example, while creatures are really related to God (in the sense that their relationship to God is part of their very being, which would disappear without him), God is not really related to his creatures: nothing would happen to him if they disappeared.[6] Ultimately he is in no way dependent on them or affected by them. They are not necessary to him—and that not merely in order for him to be what he is but even because he is what he is. There was no need for him to create—even out of love. In this as in everything else (as Karl Barth has reasserted so vehemently in our day) God is completely free. His being is wholly necessary: that of the world totally un-necessary and contingent.

[5] *The Reality of God* ... (London, 1967), p. 48; see the whole section "Toward a New Theism," pp. 44–70.
[6] *Summa Theologiae*, Ia. 13.7.

It is this doctrine of God—of a Being ultimately impassible (in the strict sense of not being able to be acted upon), eternally unaffected, for whom the world and all it stands for is finally expendable, that has proved so repugnant to atheists like Camus. And it is important to recognize that this protest is not made simply on the grounds of God's character—that, for instance, in face of the evident evil in creation such a God is morally intolerable. In this the atheist's critique is often penetrating, but it may be turned by the theist on the grounds that a God of this character is not the God he believes in. No; Camus' charge is against *any* God whose very existence makes the world we know un-necessary. Of course, he would agree that the world might not have been. But it *is*. And that is the only base from which we can start—the sheer givenness of what is. In this Camus stands solidly for a generation which believes that whatever else is real, this world at least is real. For this generation, no philosophy, no theology which does not take this conviction seriously is itself to be taken seriously. To that extent one must agree with Ogden that the God of traditional theism cannot be the God of secular man. This is not, again, to give in to secular*ism,* which holds that this world *alone* is real. But I believe that the contemporary protest against the God of theism is valid, because such theism does not start where we are.

Where "we" are can perhaps be caught best in a quotation:

If, as a result of some interior revolution, I were successively to lose my faith in Christ, my faith in a personal God, my faith in the Spirit, I think I would still continue to believe in the World. The World (the value, the infallibility, the goodness of the World): that, in the final analysis, is the first and last thing in which I believe.

These are the words not of a cosmic pantheist, nor of a Huxleyan humanist, but of a profound Christian believer of our time—Teilhard de Chardin.[7] They reveal an approach, a view of reality, which is very different from that, say, of medieval man (or, indeed, of pre-secular man generally). This does not mean that it is necessarily less Christian in any way. But it must, I am convinced, profoundly affect the manner in which we can hope to make real the centrality of the *Thou*—to ourselves or to anyone else.

Instead of postulating a necessary Being for whom the world might or might not exist, we have to begin from the sheer givenness, the isness, the thusness of the only reality we can certainly know. This is the necessary starting point, the knot in the thread, *for us,* in relation to which everything *else* is contingent. All statements about God, if we make them, are interpretations of this reality. We have to begin our thinking, even about transcendence, "from below."[8] This is *not* to say that the world = God, or that God is dependent on the world or is a mere function of it. On the contrary, the world is entirely dependent on God, the *Thou* in whom it is grounded and of whose being and activity it is the field. It is this that one is affirming when one says of everything: "In the beginning, God"—as also "in the middle, God" and "in the end, God"—"for from him and through him and to him are all things."[9] The doctrine of creation *ex nihilo* does not exist to

---

[7] *How I Believe;* quoted by H. de Lubac, *The Faith of Teilhard de Chardin* (London, 1965), p. 136, who devotes the whole of the second half of his book to a defense of this passage.

[8] See the very perceptive comments in Colin W. Williams, *Faith in a Secular Age,* pp. 39–42 and 75–89. He characterizes secular man as "concerned to understand life from within and to master life from below" (p. 112).   [9] Romans 11.36.

assert that there was a time or a state in which a Being called God was there alone and that "out of nothing" he made the world—though he might not have done. That is to indulge in a tissue of mythopoeic speculation. What it asserts is that there is nothing in the whole range of experience which cannot be interpreted in terms of God or which requires any other ground. That is to say, there is no aspect of nature or history, however resistant to personal categories, that is not *ultimately* to be seen in terms of spirit, freedom, love. From the start, affirms the believer, this is a "personalizing" universe, in the sense that the whole is to be understood as a process making for personality and beyond. The "omega point," as Teilhard de Chardin calls it, is a suprapersonal communion in which "God is all and in all," in which everything is related to the source, ground, and goal of its being in a relationship not merely of physical dependence but of spiritual interdependence.

This involves the assertion that freedom and consciousness and personality are not simply accidental productions, emergent epiphenomena, toward the end of the evolutionary process. A non-dualistic doctrine of creation involves taking creativity seriously as of ultimate significance all the way through. Whatever *more* one may want to say by insisting on transcendence, *at least* one is asserting an immanent creativity, a purposive spontaneity on the "inside of things," continuously from the beginning—so that consciousness, freedom, and personality are but making explicit what was already implicit.

There is ultimately no proof of this: it is an act of interpretation. But it is one that is borne out rather than contradicted by the direction in which biologists of very different convictions are moving—e.g. Julian Huxley, C. H. Waddington, Alister Hardy, W. H. Thorpe, as well as Teilhard de Chardin.[10] Without what John Cobb, under the influence of Whitehead, calls some "appetition" running right through creation it is difficult to explain the momentum of the process:

A stone is far more capable of survival than a plant or animal, and on the whole the lower forms of life are more readily adapted to survival than are the higher. Some other force seems to be at work in nature besides random variation and the survival of the fittest—some appetition toward more complex forms of order more difficult to sustain but more valuable in their results.[11]

The argument about the evidence I must leave to the biologists, and it can never in itself be conclusive. My concern here is rather to relate the Christian interpretation of creation to the panentheistic rather than to the theistic projection.

First, I should like to attempt to rephrase the Biblical passage which above all is trying to express the conviction that the entire process of nature and history is to be viewed not only, to use Teilhard de Chardin's categories, in terms of "hominization" but of "Christification." This will frankly be a paraphrase, not a translation, and is not meant to be

[10] It is not of final consequence for our purposes what in Teilhard is the vision of "the scientist" and what of "the seer" (to use the two categories of C. E. Raven's title: *Teilhard de Chardin, Scientist and Seer*). Any man in this area is speaking as more than a scientist, however important it may be for other purposes to differentiate more rigorously. On this see Hardy, *The Living Stream* (London, 1965), pp. 17-20; W. H. Thorpe, *Science, Man and Morals* (London, 1965), pp. 56-58; and I. G. Barbour, *Issues in Science and Religion* (London, 1966), pp. 403-8.

[11] *A Christian Natural Theology* (Philadelphia, 1965), p. 171.

taken as exegesis. But it may help to interpret what was intended to be a cosmic panorama in terms of modern evolutionary cosmology. The passage is, of course, the prologue to St. John's Gospel. Recast it might run something like this:[12]

The clue to the universe as personal was present from the beginning. It was to be found at the level of reality which we call God. Indeed, it was no other than God nor God than it. At that depth of reality the element of the personal was there from the start. Everything was drawn into existence through it, and there is nothing in the process that has come into being without it. Life owes its emergence to it, and life lights the path to man. It is that light which illumines the darkness of the subpersonal creation, and the darkness never succeeded in quenching it.

That light was the clue to reality—the light which comes to clarity in man. Even before that it was making its way in the universe. It was already in the universe, and the whole process depended upon it, although it was not conscious of it. It came to its own in the evolution of the personal; yet persons failed to grasp it. But, to those who did, who believed in what it represented, it gave the potential of a fully personal relationship to God. For these the meaning of life was seen to rest, not simply on its biological basis, nor on the impulses of nature or the drives of history, but on the reality of God. And this divine personal principle found embodiment in a man and took habitation in our midst. We saw its full glory, in all its utterly gracious reality—the wonderful sight of a person living in uniquely normal relationship to God, as son to father.

From this fulness of life we have all received, in gifts without measure. It was law that governed the less than fully personal rela-

---

[12] I have omitted the interrupting (and I am convinced, with many scholars, the originally independent) prose sections relating to John the Baptist. For the scholarly basis of this omission, see my article "The Relation of the Prologue to the Gospel of St. John," *New Testament Studies,* 9 (1963), 120–29, reprinted in S.P.C.K. Theological Collections 4, *The Authorship and Integrity of the New Testament* (London, 1965), pp. 61–72.

tionships even of man; the true, gracious reality came to expression in Jesus Christ. The ultimate reality of God no one has ever seen. But the one who has lived closest to it, in the unique relationship of son to father, he has laid it bare.

Everything was alive with his life, from the very beginning. Such is the Biblical interpretation of the creative process. The full reality was not visible in the process. Indeed, from the start and all the way through, it transcended the process: always it was "above" it, "beyond" it, drawing it upwards and onwards. In the vivid imagery of the Old Testament, the Spirit was moving or brooding over the face of the waters.[13] Even the inorganic is to be interpreted not simply in terms of life (*nephesh*) but in terms of spirit (*ruach*), of the Spirit of God drawing it out to freedom and love. For the divine action is seen not simply as an immanent purposiveness, but as a brooding over. The process is not self-activating but is always response to a Call, to a Beyond. The creative Ground is not identified with the process, like the emergent Deity in some forms of Bergsonian pantheism: the Creator is not created, God is not evolved.

It may indeed be difficult for us as men to picture the process as purposive except in the anthropomorphic myth of the *deus faber,* of the Person who plans and makes. It is incontrovertibly a Biblical image. Yet the potter and his pot (or any variation upon it) is clearly a subpersonal representation of the relationship, if not of the agent. It is not in fact how *persons* are brought into being, and we should never dream of using it as an analogy to explain to an individual how he came to be. Purely biologically, the image of fathering or begetting is obviously nearer the mark. Yet in the Christian tradition this

---

[13] Genesis I.2.

language has been reserved for the second Person of the Trinity, who, in distinction from every creature, is "begotten not made." Yet this biological imagery does not in any case take us to the heart of the matter. A human infant does not become a *person* by the process of fathering, or as a result of any purely physical nexus. It might be nearer the truth to say it is by mothering, since it is normally with the mother that the relationship of love, which draws the child out to freedom and responsibility, first begins. I am not made a person by a super-Person casting me in his own image. That is a hopelessly limited metaphor. I am made a person as the *I* of the *I-Thou* relationship is drawn out to selfhood in response to the grace and claim of the *Thou*.

And what is true of the growth of an individual to personality is more likely to be a satisfactory analogy (though it is only an analogy) for representing the evolution of the whole cosmic process to the level of personal response. Left to itself, without the personal relationships surrounding it, the human infant would never come to personhood. Without the *Thou* of another, drawing it, as it were, from beyond, it would remain at the subpersonal, biological level. In the same way, for the Biblical world-view, the universe itself is seen not in terms of a purely immanent self-developing process but as "called" into being and drawn to the level of life, personality, and spirit by the evocative lure of a love that will not let it rest. The Bible thinks of creation not in terms of emanation, in Hindu fashion, as though it were being spun—or were spinning itself—out of the body of a spider, but in terms of evocation, of its responding to a call to ever higher life and freer relationship.

I know of no more vivid expression of this than a passage from the autobiography of the Cretan writer Nikos Kazantzakis, author of *Zorba the Greek*. The language is inevitably poetic rather than scientific.

Blowing through heaven and earth, and in our hearts and the heart of every living thing, is a gigantic breath—a great Cry—which we call God. Plant life wished to continue its motionless sleep next to stagnant waters, but the Cry leaped up within it and violently shook its roots: "Away, let go of the earth, walk!" Had the tree been able to think and judge, it would have cried, "I don't want to. What are you urging me to do? You are demanding the impossible!" But the Cry, without pity, kept shaking its roots and shouting, "Away, let go of the earth, walk!"

It shouted in this way for thousands of eons; and lo! as a result of desire and struggle, life escaped the motionless tree and was liberated.

Animals appeared—worms—making themselves at home in water and mud. "We're just fine," they said. "We have peace and security; we're not budging!"

But the terrible Cry hammered itself pitilessly into their loins. "Leave the mud, stand up, give birth to your betters!"

"We don't want to! We can't!"

"You can't, but I can. Stand up!"

And lo! after thousands of eons, man emerged, trembling on his still unsolid legs.

The human being is a centaur; his equine hoofs are planted in the ground, but his body from breast to head is worked on and tormented by the merciless Cry. He has been fighting, again for thousands of eons, to draw himself, like a sword, out of his animalistic scabbard. He is also fighting—this is his new struggle—to draw himself out of his human scabbard. Man calls in despair. "Where can I go? I have reached the pinnacle, beyond is the abyss." And the Cry answers, "I am beyond. Stand up!" All things are centaurs. If this were not the case, the world would rot into inertness and sterility.[14]

---

[14] *Report to Greco* (London, 1965), pp. 291–92.

"The Cry" is both immanent and transcendent. The call is of God and the response is of God. As in the great passage of St. Paul's on the same theme, the Spirit is on both sides of the relationship, taking up the sigh of creation for fulfilment and turning it into prayer.[15] God is "the beyond" yet "in the midst" —at the heart of the process from the beginning, yet ever ahead, going on before. His is the lure of the *Thou* drawing out all things to a level of life perpetually beyond the grasp of attainment. The "how," the "mechanism" (if that is the right word), of this process, is the particular concern of the scientist, not the theologian. But the fascinating picture of the evolutionary process drawn by Sir Alister Hardy in his Gifford Lectures, *The Living Stream,* gives the layman at any rate a glimpse of how, as it were, a carpet may look from its underside. He explores the evidence not only of external natural selection operating on the physical level but increasingly, as the story advances, of internal behavioral selection on what might be called the pre-psychic level. As the species reaches out to meet the challenge of new patterns of life and environment, this leads to the development (not by the inheritance of acquired characteristics, but by the selection of the gene-mutations favorable to this habit or environment) of structures, whether of lung, wing, eye, or brain, which enable the organism to live above its previous level.

But the Biblical writers are concerned not with the detail but with the interpretation of this entire process in terms of the evocative "word" of God "calling the generations from the beginning"[16] and coming in the fullness of time to definition in Christ. And it is this that gives unity to their understanding

[15] Romans 8.14–28.   [16] Isaiah 41.4.

of the whole, in the purpose of him who is both Beginning and End, Alpha and Omega. For the same pattern can be traced throughout what we separate as nature and history, though it is interesting that the Bible is close to modern science in stressing the unbroken continuity of the two. Man does not, as we should expect, have a separate "day" of creation to himself; he shares it with all the other land animals.[17] And in the second creation story, not only is man, like everything else, formed out of dust from the ground, but the link between nature and history is symbolized in God bringing every beast and bird to Adam to be given its *name,* that is, its significance in terms of personal purpose.[18]

The God who "calls the foundations of the earth and the heavens that they stand forth together"[19] and "calls for the corn and increases it"[20] is the same God who summons Adam to response and responsibility, and above all calls out a people to himself. It is this pattern that Harvey Cox fastens on in making the point that for the Biblical writers the characteristic "place" of God, if we must localize him, is not so much "out there" in space as "ahead" of man in history.[21] God is the one who goes on before; who challenges Abraham to set forth, not knowing where he is going; who calls to Moses out of the midst of the burning bush, summoning him through the mysticism of nature in the depths of the wilderness to the politics of history in industrial Egypt, and disclosing his "ultimate" reality in the name which is as much "I

[17] Genesis 1.24–31.   [18] Genesis 2.4–24.   [19] Isaiah 48.13.
[20] Ezekiel 36.29.
[21] See *The Secular City* (especially chaps. 5 and 6); D. Callahan, ed., *The Secular City Debate*, pp. 197–203; and "The Death of God and the Future of Theology" in W. R. Miller, ed., *The New Christianity*, pp. 379–89.

will be what I will be" as "I am what I am";[22] who teaches his people to live as men who must be on their way in the morning; who precedes them in the cloud by day and the pillar of fire by night; who draws them on as pilgrims that have here no abiding city; who puts eternity into man's heart and teases him with the hope of a Messianic age.

And when the Messiah does come, he still calls men out to a kingdom which within history is always "at hand," to a quality of living that always eludes their grasp. Constantly it is there before them,[23] just as he himself is on the road ahead,[24] urging them to follow. And even at what appears to be the end, he again goes on before them, first into Galilee, and then to the ends of the earth and the end of time.

Once more the process starts afresh in the apostolic Church. Its whole life is directed toward the *parousia,* or presence, of Christ, viewed not as a static, appropriated reality, but as a constant coming into the midst. And St. Paul's final testimony is typical of the craning hope on which the Bible closes: "I do not consider that I have made it my own; but one thing I do, forgetting what lies behind and straining forward to what lies ahead, I press on toward the goal for the prize of the upward call of God in Christ Jesus."[25] "I am not yet perfect," he says: yet the Christian's calling is to be *teleios,*[26] which means fundamentally not one who is morally perfect but one whose entire life is moulded by the *telos* or end of God in Christ.

This has led us from the God of nature to the God of history, from the doctrine of creation to the doctrine of God's dealing

---

[22] Exodus 3.14.
[23] The force of the verb in Matthew 12.28 = Luke 11.20.
[24] Mark 10.32.   [25] Philippians 3.13–14.   [26] Matthew 5.48.

with men in providence and miracle. The distinctive feature
of the Biblical record is that he is indeed the God of history
and not merely of nature, the God who acts, in contrast to the
Baalim of the nature religions or the Brahman of Hinduism.
And yet the *representation* of this indispensable personal quality in traditional theism has tended to discredit the very thing
it is most concerned to safeguard. God has been pictured as a
super-Self, deciding to act, intervene, or send this, that, or the
other, including his own "Son." As anthropomorphic myth,
this is easy on the human imagination, and of course those
who use this language are readily prepared to admit the "as
if." But the projection it employs has the effect of locating the
action of God as a Being outside, behind, or between the
processes of nature and history. It gives men today little help
toward seeing him as the inside *of* these processes. In consequence it has the opposite result of confirming them in belief
in a system of scientific humanism closed to such eternal in-
terference. Somehow we must find a projection which enables
us to represent the divine initiative as *in* the processes of nature rather than as acting on them from without, as exer-
cised through the events of secular history rather than in some
sacred super-history.

There is at this point a very real hangover of thinking to be
overcome which goes back to the notion of God that received
its classic expression in deism. This requires, psychologically,
that the distinctive action of God be marked by at least an apparent suspension or overruling of what would otherwise
happen "in the natural course of events." Teilhard de Chardin
alludes to this in relation to the presumption that the appearance of the first man must represent a special, discontinuous

act of creation (although, as we have seen, the Bible does not even give it a "day" to itself):

Many people suppose that the superiority of spirit would be "jeopardized" if its first manifestation were not accompanied by some interruption of the normal advance of the world. One ought rather to say that precisely because it is spirit its appearance must take the form of a crowning achievement, or a blossoming. But leaving aside all thought of systematization, is it not true that every day a multitude of human souls are created in the course of an embryogenic process in which scientific observation will never be able to detect any break however small in the chain of biological phenomena? Thus we have daily before our eyes an example of an act of creation which is absolutely imperceptible to, and beyond the reach of, science as such. Why then make so many difficulties when it is a question of the first man?[27]

One could naturally go on to ask the same question, to which he might not have given so easy an answer, of the appearance of "the Christ." Why should this require a discontinuity of germ-plasm? I do not wish in this book to enter the field of what are properly Christological questions. But the presupposition that the uniqueness of Christ, like the uniqueness of man (whatever we may mean by each of these), *depends upon* a special divine intervention is part of the doctrine of God, not Christ. This is in no way to deny that there could have been or was such a special act. What must be disputed is that the theological truth of the Virgin Birth depends upon, or indeed consists of, a belief in a biological discontinuity. It is possible to believe that Jesus' entire life, from conception to death and beyond, was indeed "of the Holy Spirit," and yet to regard the culminating answer of sonship to which creation points as

[27] Quoted in the collection of *pensées* in *Hymn of the Universe*, pp. 100–1.

given *through* the nexus of heredity and environment rather than as possible only by their breach and supersession. Indeed, I believe that one of the most important functions of a contemporary doctrine of God is precisely to *safeguard this possibility,* not only in relation to the Virgin Birth, but also in relation to the miracles and resurrection of Jesus. I am convinced as any of the theological truth which these represent, and have no wish to depreciate or deny them. But I am equally convinced that, if this truth is made to depend on or is equated with suspension of the physical processes, then men are being asked to give assent to something different from the heart of the Biblical gospel. For faith for the New Testament is *not* belief in the occurrence of a physical miracle, but trust in the utterly gracious action and presence of God in Christ. This is the *miraculum*—the wonderful thing —the sheer, overwhelming sense of the *Thou* of God meeting us in particular events or particular persons. Nothing in the New Testament *requires* (though equally nothing excludes) the belief that these events or persons also represent a break or discontinuity in the stream of life. To speak as though it does is to confound the categories, to insist that the reality of the *Thou* can be represented only by certain configurations or lacunae in the world of *It.*

This, I would stress, is in no way to prejudge the evidence— for instance, with regard to the Empty Tomb (which I hold to be strong) or with regard to the Virgin Birth (which is considerably weaker). I am not discussing that here. I am solely concerned with the presumption, carried over from a particular (supranaturalistic) projection of the divine reality, that belief in the personal initiative of God in history necessarily demands a certain way of representing his action. But one has only to use the phrase "personal initiative" to suggest the idea of "intervention" or, conversely, to deny "intervention" to be assumed to have an impersonal doctrine of God. Such is the long shadow of deism from which theism has never quite escaped.

The same holds of the doctrine of providence, which is essentially the assertion that in, through, and under every event there is to be seen the grace and claim of the *Thou*, the personal reality of God from whose love literally nothing can separate. God is "in" everything from the hairs on a head to the fall of a sparrow. Yet the very mention of "providence," let alone of "special providence" (which is only asserting the utterly personal quality of this gracious presence for the subject-in-relationship), brings up the notion of some divine manipulator who disposes the mechanism of events to produce a result that would otherwise not have occurred, or who dispenses blessings, or curses, in the lives of individuals or groups. The concept of a "disposer supreme" who, like some celestial Mikado, so works everything that all turns out for the best in the best of all possible worlds (otherwise God could not be both good and all-powerful) dies very hard. In its extreme form this expresses itself in the conviction that somewhere there is a Planner and Purposer who sees that every accident is no accident and fits each effect to its cause to accomplish his grand design. But it is widely—and not unjustifiably—believed that everything that happens to an individual is held by the theist to be intended or "meant," and that to question this is *ipso facto* to question belief in a personal God.

But this correlation between personal providence and planned intent is, I believe, a consequence of the particular projection (found in deism and theism) of God as a Father-figure or Super-ego designing and directing the operation of the world from above. What essentially the Christian faith is asserting is that in and through all the processes of nature and history there is a personal outcome to be traced and a love to be met which nothing can finally defeat. It does not necessarily imply that these processes are themselves the deliberate expression of willed intention, any more than are the millions of physical and psychological reactions which in human beings form the raw material of personal purpose. It is not that "all things work together for good," or that God deliberately "works" all things thus, by some super-computerized design, but rather that "in everything ... he [the Spirit] co-operates for good with those who love God"[28]—that is to say, for those who make the response of love, in every concatenation of circumstance, however pointless[29] and indeed intentionless, there is to be met the graciousness of a *Thou* capable of transforming and liberating even the most baffling and opaque into meaning and purpose.

All this is intimately connected, as in Romans 8, with the problem of evil. It is not my intention, at the end of a chapter, to launch into a full discussion of this inexhaustible theme. The classical treatments of the problem of evil in Christian theology have tended to push the answer either back to a primeval past or forward to an eschatological future. If this were the choice, I would side with John Hick in his *Evil and the God of Love* in preferring the latter. But I agree with H. A. Williams in feeling that neither is really any answer at all.[30] The problem lies in how we relate evil to our conception

[28] Romans 8.28 (N.E.B.).   [29] The "vanity" of Romans 8.20.
[30] *The God I Want*, edited by James Mitchell (London, 1967), pp. 183–90. Williams' own thinking moves in much the same direction as mine.

of God in the present. And once again it seems to me that here is an area in which there has been serious displacement in the theistic projection. All I can say is that the traditional presentation of the problem fails to locate it for me and that its attempt to justify the ways of God to men is strangely irrelevant, if not grotesque. Confronted by a personal tragedy or a large-scale disaster it never really occurs to me to regard it as the work of a Being who "allows" (let alone "sends") such terrible things. If, for instance, a person for whom I cared deeply were killed in a plane crash or were found to have an inoperable cancer, I should find it wholly unnatural to blame a divine Planner or to disbelieve in his existence because of it. For in these things there is not intentionality (apart from any possible human factor). They have not been willed or planned for the individual concerned. Nor are they *against* God's will, as if he were merely at their mercy and had been frustrated by blind factors or other wills. God is *in* the cancer as he is in the sunset, and is to be met and responded to in each. Both are among the faces of God, the one terrible, the other beautiful. Neither as such is the face of love, but, as in the Cross for the Christian, even the worst can be transformed and "vanquished." The "problem" of evil is not how God can will it (that is not even touched on in Romans 8), but its power to threaten meaninglessness and separation, to sever and to sour, and to darken our capacity to make the response of *Thou.*

If this is the case, then the first task for theology is to restate the problem rather than to look for a solution. So much of the conventional presentation of the problem of evil, both from the Christian and the anti-Christian side, assumes a Being who is "personally responsible" for directing the course of events so as to produce the distribution of suffering we see, or even "visiting" individuals with occurrences in which they should be able to detect "the hand of God." Such a Being is declared by the atheist to be morally intolerable, and I find myself concurring. Any human planner who foresaw, let alone designed, a flood or a landslide, would evacuate the area beforehand. I have no wish to defend such a conception of God, and presentations of the problem of evil, however poignant, which state it in this form, fail, in my experience, to engage. One senses the genuine agony that lies behind the discussion, say, of the innocent suffering of a child, but to define the problem in terms of how this can be "meant," and therefore justified, in terms of an almighty Being who permits it, is to distort the issue from the beginning. Yet such is the effect of traditional theism.

Once again, it seems to me, we have to start from the other end. The concatenation of events that produces earthquakes and accidents, the cruelties of natural selection and the indiscriminate sufferings of war, are not to be seen in terms of prevenient intention. That is to introduce categories of interpretation as foreign as those of the old teleologists who argued that fleas were made black so that men could see to swat them against white sheets. Taking the immanence, the incarnation, of God seriously as the form or field of his transcendence, as the panentheistic projection does, means that categories of intentionality and the like are relevant only when the Divine is operating through personality.[31] In the dense world of subpersonal relationships (which includes all but the self-conscious tip of human life, as well as the rest of nature), the purposiveness of love works itself out through "blinder" cate-

---

[31] Jung speaks of God's "unconsciousness" and reminds us that of the four "faces" of the living creatures round the throne of God in Ezekiel and Revelation only one is human (*The Collected Works,* XI, 416 and 383).

gories. There is no *intention* in an earthquake or an accident. But in and through it it is still possible to respond to the *Thou* that claims even this for meaning and personal purpose. Everything can be taken up and transformed rather than allowed to build up into a dark patch of loveless resentment and meaningless futility.

Such is the message of the remarkable passages from *Incognito* quoted earlier. God is in everything and not merely in the obviously good and meaningful. This is the significance of the words, "I form light and create darkness, I make weal and create woe, I am the Lord, who do all these things,"[32] which make God such a Devil if they are understood in terms of intentionality. In this, panentheism takes its stand against the dualism of theism, moral as well as metaphysical. But it does not side with the indifferentism of pantheism, which has to maintain that evil is in some way illusory or unreal. The evil in the world is indeed terrifyingly real, both at the subpersonal and at the personal level; but it is still part of the face of *God*.[33] That is to say, love is there to be met and to be created through it and out of it. It is not without purpose: meaning can be wrested from it even at the cost of crucifixion. It is not separate from the face of love, and therefore cannot separate from it. That is the saving grace: God is not outside evil any more than he is outside anything else, and the promise is that he *"will* be all in all" *as love*. And that, in Christ, is the ultimate truth of everything *now*, however hidden or obscured.

[32] Isaiah 45.7.
[33] This recognition receives moving, if at times perverse, expression in Jung's *Answer to Job* and at the end of his earlier work *A Psychological Approach to the Dogma of the Trinity*.

CHAPTER SIX

The Journey Inwards

*The longest journey
Is the journey inwards.*[1]

In the last analysis the way of exploration into God is the way of prayer. It is not an exercise in theology. And yet theology can have the effect of seriously distorting the map. And nowhere perhaps is the effect more powerful than in the area of prayer itself.

This chapter is in no sense a treatise on the spiritual life, let alone a conducted tour into the interior. It has a more modest aim. It is concerned with the hindering of hindrances. For I am coming to be convinced that in this area the very word "prayer" may be suffering for large numbers of people the same displacement and loss of reality as the word "God"—and for the same reasons. For "prayer" is equated with making contact with this Being who has ceased to be anything but peripheral to men's deepest sense of reality. Just as he is no longer the *ens realissimum,* and, as God, is dead, so prayer has become a dead area for vast numbers of our contemporaries.

Within the Church this is accompanied by a great sense of largely unadmitted guilt. I am sure that large numbers both

---

[1] Dag Hammarskjöld, *Markings* (London, 1964), p. 65.

of clergy and laity have simply given up praying, in the sense in which they feel they have been taught to do so. They are consciously or unconsciously aware that they *ought* to be finding reality in something they are not. Equally, in the field of public worship they are going along with forms of service and patterns of address to the Almighty which have largely become emptied of reality but which tradition tells them are what worship is. And because, like those canvassed in the public opinion polls, they are clinging to some reality, they refuse to let go altogether.

But outside the Church I wonder how far the word "prayer" connects with what is most real, or is felt ought to be most real, at all. Just as there is an unbelievable percentage of people who say they still believe in God, so there is an astonishingly high number who still claim to pray "regularly." Again, this is testimony to something they will not let go, if only as a lifeline. But if one starts at the other end, from what *is* most real for them, one finds a rather different picture.

This was brought home to me by an experience from which it would be entirely unscientific to generalize, but which I instance simply as a pointer. I had been conducting a somewhat "offbeat" retreat for ordinands, which started not from addresses by me but from asking them to write down what they felt to be their deepest personal need. In this company and context it was accepted as natural that many, though by no means all, of the questions raised fell within the field of what would be called "spirituality." Indeed, what lay behind my intention in beginning this way was to discover what were the real questions about prayer that were exercising them, instead of imposing on them what I thought edifying.

As a result of this experiment I thought I would try it on

another group—this time of people who had written to me as a result of *Honest to God*, who were either "insiders" hanging on by the skin of their teeth or "outsiders" to the Church who wished they need not be. They had already been to a previous such gathering. So this gave the opportunity of going deeper, of trying to get down to the things that lay beneath the surface. I explained the purpose of the weekend to them in the invitation, quoting from the letter I had sent the ordinands, and speaking of it as a sort of experimental "secular retreat." At the end of the first evening I asked them to put down the questions they would most like to see tackled under the general headings of "What is my own deepest need?," "What is the deepest need of the world in which I move?," and "How are these related?" By the last session I ventured to remark that not one of the questions had touched on the subject of prayer or spirituality, nor had it once been introduced into the discussion. The reaction was interesting. It brought out that the very process of digging down into the things that *did* concern them most (and the discovery that it was possible in the freedom of such a fellowship to bare their need for communication at real depth) was to them a way into the spiritual life, or life at the level of spirit, which they refused to believe was not prayer. Indeed, because this was a genuine spiritual reality, its articulation in terms of a Communion service on the Sunday—particularly at the point of absolutely free and open intercession—obviously meant a very great deal. Yet both the word "prayer" and still more the prospect of a church service would have been a complete deterrent in advance. If I had phrased the invitation in terms of "How can we learn to pray?," rather than "What is your deepest need?," it would not, I think, have occurred to them that learning to pray was a need, any more than "their deepest need" had for them any association with "prayer." The two simply belonged to different worlds.

How is it possible to restore a link? Here again I believe it is largely a question of the projection which is used. The word "prayer" in popular usage is immediately connected with praying "to" a Being, who seems, if not to have nothing to do with the case, at any rate to be peripheral to the real issue, except perhaps *in extremis*. He does not seem to come into the question of living life to its fullest. Prayer is commended as a great "venture" or even "adventure," but because of the projection with which it is associated it does not appear to most people to beckon them in a direction in which they believe the exploration of reality lies. The invitation seems to take them out of life rather than more deeply into it. How do we reverse this?

The starting point, I am sure, is the recognition, common to all, that prayer has to do with life at its most personal—which means not simply with relationships between persons, but with response to all reality as *Thou*. It is the point at which all life (and the Bible has no hesitation in extending the attitude of "worship" to the whole of creation) responds to the claim of the Voice, the Cry, the *Thou*—the claim to live at the level of the spirit, to refuse to be content with the surface determinisms of the *It* world, but to be open to the "beyond," the creative "interior" of love, at the center of everything. Worship is the response to him who is "above all and through all and in all."[2] It is seeing all in God and God in all. Anything that discloses, or penetrates through to, this level of

---

[2] Ephesians 4.6.

reality, whether corporately or in solitude, whether in talk or action or silence, is prayer.

Prayer is opening oneself to the claim of the unconditional as it meets one in all the relationships of life. It is life at its most intimate, intense, and demanding, requiring the response of the whole person. "For the *I* of the primary-word *I-Thou* is a different *I* from that of the primary word *I-It*."[3] The pray-er is different from the user, the communer from the commuter. He is giving himself to reality at the level of ultimate rather than of proximate concern. Such a relationship can only be described in categories of *Thou,* not of *It.* And in human experience this is supremely defined in, though not confined to, response to another person.

Hence it is entirely natural that the reality of God should be *expressed as* the grace and claim of another Person. As a myth, as a projection, the description of God as *a Person,* encountered and addressed in prayer, is an entirely legitimate way of putting it. It is the simplest possible aid to the human imagination. Indeed, for most people most of the time (at any rate in the West) it is impossible to conceive of prayer except as talking to an invisible Person. Certainly this is a point at which the language of "as if" gets a great deal nearer to the heart of the reality than the language of "so what."[4] To analyze prayer, as Van Buren does,[5] simply in terms of what produces a comparable effect (e.g. supplying irrigation instead of praying for rain) is likely to kill it far more effectively than any dangers from the other side.

Nevertheless it is essential, if imagery is not to become

[3] Buber, *I and Thou,* p. 3.
[4] See above, pp. 69–70.
[5] *The Secular Meaning of the Gospel,* pp. 188–90.

idolatry, that the "as if" should not be forgotten—so that prayer becomes *defined* as "talking to God." And above all it is necessary to ask whether there may not be at least as much hindrance as help in this image, however inescapable.

I believe in fact that the theistic projection by which the reality of God is represented by the existence of "another" Person is the most powerful factor in prayer's going dead in the way that I have described. For the Christian it creates a conflict and sense of guilt because this is how he has been taught that God *ought* to be real to him. For the non-Christian, it makes prayer, so far from being a way *into* reality, seem—if anything—to be an escape from it. Prayer appears to be a means of leaving the world (even if only to return to it) in order to "be with God."

Moreover, however much one tries to avoid it, the theistic projection encourages the personalistic interventionist conception of the divine working described in the last chapter. The God who "answers" prayers or "makes" people well again is inevitably seen as disposing the events of nature and history or the lives of individuals in a way which envisages him as standing above the processes, manipulating them from the outside. What we need is a conception of prayer that organically relates the processes themselves to the depths of the divine creativity and love. As Alister Hardy puts it:

Instead of supposing that one great personal-like Deity is thinking out simultaneously the detailed answers to millions of different problems of all the individuals in the world, is it not more reasonable to suppose that some action is set in motion by prayer which draws the particular solution for each one of us from our own subconscious minds? In saying this I must again make clear that I am not implying that I believe this destroys our conception of the Divine. All the evidence of religious experience, I believe, shows that man makes contact with this Power which appears partly transcendent, and is felt as the numinous beyond the self, and partly immanent within him. I also think it likely, however, that it may well be this uplifting power which does in fact activate the subconscious solution-providing mechanism in a way which would not otherwise be possible. In a similar way it may be the same power which assists in the healing of a sick person.[6]

But, above all, the highly personalistic theistic model of prayer and worship may subtly become an escape from the very personal reality it is designed to safeguard and express. The essence of prayer is opening ourselves to the grace and claim of the unconditional as it meets us in, through, and under the finite relationships of life. It is allowing ourselves to be met and addressed by the *Thou*. And common or corporate prayer, as the Christian understands it, is the *sharing* of this ultimate concern, exposing ourselves together to be sensitized, deepened, built up in the awareness of *agape* love as the ground of all our lives. It involves meeting, sharing at the deepest level, in the *koinonia* of Holy Spirit. It means listening and confessing to each other, making corporate response and commitment to that which encounters us in Christ. By its very nature it is a "face-to-face" activity in which evasion of the *Thou* is by definition impossible.

And yet, as we know only too well, worship can easily become the very opposite of this, a face-to-back activity, in which one can take part without really meeting or even speaking to anyone; and so-called "Holy" Communion can become a substitute for real communion. There are doubtless many reasons for this having to do with human fears and failings, but I think it has to be recognized that one of

[6] *The Divine Flame* (London, 1966), p. 236.

the most effective mechanisms of this evasion is precisely the bringing in of the unseen Person and the addressing of ourselves to *him* in the presence of the others. By thus "turning" to God in prayer, it is easy to substitute the *Thou* we cannot see for the *Thous* through whom the claim meets us. The special diction of prayer (in which we should never address *each other*) assists us to direct our response out and away, beyond the east wall, to the other end of each individual telephone wire—anywhere to avoid being confronted by the beyond in the midst "between man and man." And in intercession the "telstar" image of prayer, by which, as it were, messages for others are redirected off a heavenly Being, can make for effective escape from direct communication—or action. Concern for the everyday world of the newspapers is translated into "prayer" by the introduction of some such circumlocution as "O Lord, thou knowest . . ."; and it is when the *Thou* addressed in the ordinary responses of life *gives way* to the *Thou* of God that "worship" is usually held to begin.

These are not, of course, necessary implications of the theistic projection of God as a separate Person *to* whom prayer is addressed *from* the world. Indeed, they would properly be rejected, and probably resented, as distortions. But they are such common *accompaniments* as at least to raise the question whether this projection does not do as much harm as it undoubtedly does good.

But what of an alternative projection? In a real sense there is no need to look for one. For there is an already existing alternative in the mystical tradition, which, both inside and outside the Christian Church, has worked with a very different model. A useful conspectus of this tradition is readily accessible in F. C. Happold's anthology, *Mysticism*; and, except where I have indicated otherwise, the brief excerpts I have taken from original sources can all be checked in their context there. What, then, are the characteristics of this model of the spiritual life?

In the first place, there is no doubt that the mystics, without by any means being pure immanentists or pantheists, have worked with a projection which locates God at what St. John of the Cross calls "the deep center." "The journey inwards" is sufficiently indicated by Boehme's invitation: "Gather in all thy thoughts and by faith press into the Center"; for "God is more inward to us than we are to ourselves" (Ruysbroeck); "God is nearer to us than our own soul; for he is the ground in whom our soul standeth" (Mother Julian). Meister Eckhart employs the same analogy from cosmology that we used before:

Suppose one dropped a millstone from the sun to earth, the earth being pierced straight through the center, the millstone would stop falling at the center of the earth. Here is the heart of the earth, the stopping-place of everything on earth. So is the Trinity the stopping-place of creatures as a whole.

Yet even so extreme an immanentist as Eckhart never *identifies* God with the depths of the soul. While God can plumb to the bottom of the soul, the soul can never exhaust the depths of God. On the one hand,

God enters the ground of the soul. None can touch the ground of the soul but God only.

Yet, on the other hand,

Though she [the soul] sink all sinking in the oneness of divinity she never touches bottom. Wherefore God has left her one little point from which to get back to herself and find herself and know herself as creature. For it is of the very essence of the soul that she is powerless to plumb the depths of her creator.

The language of the mystics is that of "transcendence *within* immanence,"[7] of union without the abolition of distinction, of identification without identity, of a "coinherence" of the divine Spirit with the human, of "a presence...far more deeply interfused."[8] It is the language of what Thomas R. Kelly, the American Quaker, in a modern classic, *A Testament of Devotion,* calls "infused prayer," with its "awareness of a more-than-ourselves, working persuadingly and powerfully at the roots of our own soul, and in the depths of all men." "We are joyfully *prayed through,*" he says, "by a Seeking Life that flows through us into the world of men."[9]

Yet though the projection is encouraging, what of the reality mapped? How far is it "the God and Father of our Lord Jesus Christ"? Certainly, it is hardly that in Wordsworth, valid as his vision may be. How far can mysticism be true to the personal, the historical, the incarnational element in the Christian awareness of God? And above all does it begin to satisfy the worldly, secular approach upon which we previously insisted with equal emphasis? It is the apparent absence of this from the mystical tradition which has caused many, including myself, to suspect it. Indeed, temperamentally I should have said that I was the least mystical of persons, just as I am the least musical and the least psychic. It is not that I am uninterested in these aspects of reality: I find them fascinating. But if, as has been suggested, there are two spiritual types, the mystical and the prophetic, then I should have to align myself with the prophetic.

[7] I take the phrase from A. C. Bouquet's "Numinous Uneasiness," *The Modern Churchman,* April 1966, p. 206; quoted by H. A. Williams in J. Mitchell, ed., *The God I Want,* p. 177.

[8] W. Wordsworth, "Tintern Abbey."

[9] (London, 1957), p. 39.

For there is far too strong an element to be fortuitous in the mystical tradition which is anti-historical, anti-temporal, acosmic. It involves a turning away from the multiplicity, the individuality, the flux of phenomena—all that the Hindu sums up as *maya* or the Buddhist as *samsara*. It tends to make for detachment rather than involvement, for indifference rather than commitment, and there is a strong emphasis on purgation, renunciation, mortification—on "forgetting all outward things" (Richard of St. Victor).

The following excerpts are far from atypical:

Three things prevent a man from knowing God at all. The first is time, the second corporality, and the third is multiplicity or number. As long as these three things are in me God is not in me nor is he working in me really (Eckhart).

Learn to turn from worldly things, and give yourself to spiritual things, and you will see the Kingdom of God come within you (Thomas à Kempis).

The soul does this [namely, has knowledge of itself, which is the prerequisite of all "knowledge of spiritual things"] when it is so recollected and detached from all earthly preoccupations and from the influence of the senses that it understands itself as it is in its own nature, taking no account of the body (Walter Hilton).

And, finally, there is the terrifying section on detachment in St. John of the Cross which includes the words:

Strive to go about seeking not the best of temporal things, but the worst. Strive thus to desire to enter into complete detachment and emptiness and poverty, with respect to everything that is in the world, for Christ's sake.[10]

---

[10] *The Ascent of Mount Carmel*, I.13.

It is hardly surprising that the mystics have had a limited appeal. Yet I am not convinced that this one-sided anti-worldliness is of the essence of their contribution. It belongs partly to a Manichean world-denying strain that entered Christian mysticism through Plotinus and Pseudo-Dionysius. It belongs also to a pre-scientific, pre-humanist, pre-industrial age in which, if one cannot master the world, the only thing to do is to forsake it or try to forget it. No mystic writing today in fact uses *that* language.

But all along there has also been another, cosmic mysticism in which "Creatures are a guide and a path unto God and Eternity. Thus this world is an outer court of Eternity, and therefore it may well be called a Paradise, for it is such in truth" (*Theologia Germanica*). It is a tradition, which like acosmic mysticism, spreads across the boundaries of all religions. It is represented by the *Bhagavad Gita* in Hinduism, by Zen in Buddhism, by the Sufis in Mohammedanism, and by the Chasidim in Judaism who so influenced Martin Buber. Within Christianity, W. H. Auden makes the interesting observation that it is characteristic of the northern rather than the Mediterranean countries,[11] and so it seems to be.[12] For all their differences, it is possible to recognize

[11] *The Protestant Mystics,* edited by Anne Fremantle (London, 1964), Introduction by W. H. Auden, pp. 15f.

[12] It would always be possible, of course, to find exceptions—e.g. the intense nature-spirit-mysticism of Kazantzakis: "I closed my eyes, soothed. A quiet, mysterious pleasure took possession of me—as if all that green miracle around me were paradise itself, as if all the freshness, airiness and sober rapture which I was feeling were God. God changes his appearance every second. Blessed is the man who can recognize him in all his disguises. At one moment he is a glass of fresh water, the next your son bouncing on your knees or an enchanting woman, or perhaps merely a morning walk.

Little by little, everything around me, without changing shape, became

a common strain that links Mother Julian, Brother Lawrence, George Fox, Thomas Traherne, William Blake, William Wordsworth, Richard Jefferies, George Macdonald, Johannes Anker-Larsen,[13] and Pierre Teilhard de Chardin. Within this tradition one should mention also the long-standing contribution of Eastern Orthodox and Quaker spirituality, represented respectively in recent years by Nicolas Berdyaev and Petru Dumitriu[14] and by Rufus Jones and Thomas Kelly.[15] The difference from the previous type is sufficiently illustrated by two brief quotations:

Keep contact with the outer world of sense and meanings.... Walk and talk and work and laugh with your friends.[16]

The way to God lies through love of people, and there is no other way.[17]

Yet even here there are limitations to be overcome. There are two main forms of this more earthy spirituality, which are sometimes distinguished as nature-mysticism and love-mysticism. In the former there is a strong impersonal streak, represented so hauntingly in Wordsworth:

---

a dream. I was happy. Earth and paradise were one. A flower in the fields with a large drop of honey in its center: that was how life appeared to me. And my soul, a wild bee plundering" (*Zorba the Greek* [Oxford, 1959], p. 213).

[13] A Danish novelist, selections from whose writings appear in *The Protestant Mystics,* pp. 303–12.

[14] See also *Orthodox Spirituality,* by A Monk of the Eastern Church, and, for a moving practical outworking of it, Sergei Hackel, *One of Great Price: The Life of Mother Maria Skobtsova, Martyr of Ravensbrück.*

[15] See also *Christian Faith and Practice in the Experience of the Society of Friends* and H. Loukes, *The Quaker Contribution.*

[16] Kelly, *A Testament of Devotion,* p. 34.

[17] Hackel, *One of Great Price* (London, 1965), p. 29.

A motion and a spirit, that impels
All thinking things, all objects of all thoughts,
And rolls through all things. Therefore am I still
A lover of the meadows and the woods.[18]

In so far as human beings come into this mysticism, it is as part of the cycle of nature,

Rolled round in earth's diurnal course,
With rocks, and stones, and trees.[19]

Civilization and the city, with its "dark Satanic mills," are the enemy, as they were for Blake and later for D. H. Lawrence. And even in the personalizing mysticism of Teilhard de Chardin there is the honest admission that "other people" are much more like hell than heaven:

I find no difficulty in integrating into my inward life everything above me and beneath me...in the universe—whether matter, plants, animals; and then powers, dominions and angels: these I can accept without difficulty.... But "the other man," my God— by which I do not mean "the poor, the halt, the lame and the sick," but "the other" quite simply as "other," the one who seems to exist independently of me because his universe seems closed to mine, and who seems to shatter the unity and the silence of the world for me—would I be sincere if I did not confess that my instinctive reaction is to rebuff him? and that the mere thought of entering into spiritual communication with him disgusts me?[20]

It is this relationship with "the other" simply as "other" which is in fact the foundation of the "love-mysticism" of which Buber is the towering representative. And it includes rather than excludes a rapport with nature, represented for

[18] "Tintern Abbey."
[19] "A Slumber Did My Spirit Steal."
[20] *Le Milieu Divin*, p. 138.

instance in the *I-Thou* relationship with a tree which Buber describes so memorably.[21] Yet even this love-mysticism has a tendency to limitation. It is not for nothing that the more recent "secular" theologians tend to depreciate, or at any rate to find themselves in the opposite camp to, the personalists and those who emphasize the centrality of the *I-Thou* relation. For there is always a tendency (more in some of his followers than in Buber himself)[22] to regard the entire "world of systems,"[23] with its inescapable translation of love into justice and the necessity for organization and politics, as the enemy of true, personal existence. It is fair to say that what Harvey Cox notes as some of the "saving" features of life in "the secular city,"[24] its very impersonality and anonymity and mobility, its pragmatism and profanity, are among the aspects of life which "love-mysticism" would instinctively regard as destructive of spirit. The "switchboard" and the "cloverleaf" taken by Cox as the city's symbols are, to say the least, not central to the "style" of the mystics. Cox is the first to admit that "well-intentioned forays against the 'depersonalization of urban life' " are fed by a *misunderstanding* of Buber's *I-Thou* philosophy; but he thinks Buber opened the door for this by neglecting a theology of the *I-You* relationship: "The danger with an *I-Thou* typology is that all relationships which are not deeply personal and significant tend to be swept or shoved into the *I-It* category."[25] In fact, as we saw earlier, John Macmurray has worked with a threefold classification—into the instrumental, the functional, and

---

[21] *I and Thou*, pp. 7–8.
[22] See some of the very social concerns treated in *Between Man and Man*.
[23] As Brunner calls it in his *Justice and the Social Order*.
[24] *The Secular City*, chaps. 2 and 3.
[25] *Ibid.*, pp. 44, 48–49.

the personal relationship[26]—and Berdyaev was acutely aware of the need for a way of thinking that saw the answer to the "they" not simply in terms of the individual but of the "we."

Berdyaev, in fact, probably comes as near as anyone to the theological synthesis we are seeking. He was already, before the last war, talking of the "new spirituality"[27] and Chapter 6 of *Spirit and Reality,* "Mysticism: Its Contradictions and Achievements," is a penetrating analysis of precisely the problem of whether mysticism can be a valid answer to the question of "a whole spirituality."[28] He ventures to affirm a "prophetic mysticism." This is not only a mysticism of love, which makes personality, freedom, and love central, but is almost a mysticism of justice, including within it an active engagement in the social, political, and economic order. Of this social mystery he writes: "There are two symbols, bread and money; and there are two mysteries, the eucharistic mystery of bread and the satanic mystery of money. We are faced with a great task: to overthrow the rule of money and to establish in its place the rule of bread."[29] The aim can be nothing less than "a spiritual permeation of the world in order to inspire and transfigure it."[30]

"This," he recognizes, "will involve the appearance of a new type of saint, who will take upon himself the burden of

[26] See especially *Interpreting the Universe.*

[27] The title of chap. 7 of *Spirit and Reality.*

[28] Cf. his earlier *Freedom and the Spirit,* chap. 7.

[29] *Spirit and Reality,* p. 178.

[30] *Ibid.,* p. 164. He must be one of the few mystics to make central the inescapably social category of the kingdom of God (pp. 165–66). Most confine themselves to citing the highly ambiguous text "The kingdom of heaven is within you" (Luke 17.21), which is just as likely to mean "among" or "between" you. In any case, the pronoun is plural.

the complex world."[31] This is exactly the type of sainthood that Petru Dumitriu is exploring in *Incognito* (and, less successfully, in his subsequent *Westward Lies Heaven*), and which is epitomized in the moving portrait of the modern suffering servant sketched in the closing paragraphs of Pierre Berton's *The Comfortable Pew*.[32] It is the spirituality which George McLeod pleads for in his chapter on prayer in *Only One Way Left*, and which is summed up in Dag Hammarskjöld's dictum: "In our era, the road to holiness necessarily passes through the world of action."[33]

At what *stage* it passes through the world of action is no doubt partly a matter of temperament. I quoted earlier the remark of Bonhoeffer's that man's life is lived as much from the outside in as from the inside out. It is probably true that most men's lives have always been lived more from the outside in than *vice versa*. And this is particularly true of secular man. Yet the mystic has tended to be the type who lives from the inside out, and therefore to be regarded as the exception who is "not for us." This contrast comes out explicitly in Ruysbroeck. After saying that "God is more inward to us than we are to ourselves," he goes on:

And therefore God works in us from within outwards; but all creatures work from without inwards. And thus it is that grace, and all the gifts of God, and the Voice of God, come from within, in the unity of our spirit; and not from without, into the imagination, by means of sensible images.

Happold makes the observation that "in the poets the movement is usually from the *without* to the *within*; in the

---

[31] *Ibid.*, p. 99.
[32] (London, 1966), pp. 143–44.
[33] *Markings*, p. 108.

contemplatives always from the *within* to the *without*."[34] I would question the "always." Or perhaps it is a matter of how one defines "contemplative." For I believe there is truth in George McLeod's suggestion that for our time it may be necessary for most people who are not "religious" in the technical, monastic sense, to *invert* the traditional stages of contemplative mysticism—the purgative, the illuminative, the unitive.[35] It is by "a deeper immersion in existence" (Kierkegaard), rather than by beginning with detachment, that most people today, I believe, are likely to experience the "pressure and the wounding" (Hamilton) of the presence of God. Caught up in the solidarities of involvement, they may then find themselves driven to what Berdyaev calls the "asceticism" of "action in the world,"[36] of stripping down, con-centration. The traditional approach has been to start at the center and then go out, to begin with prayer and "work it out" in politics. This approach may be reversed for our generation, with so many of its most articulate and responsible members heavily committed to such involvements as the Freedom Movement, the struggle against poverty, over-population, and war, and the revolution for "tomorrow's sun"[37] that lies so close beneath the horizon of the southern hemisphere. Perhaps today most things begin in politics and end in mysticism, rather than the other way round. At any

---

[34] F. C. Happold, *Mysticism, A Study and Anthology* (Harmondsworth, Eng., 1963), p. 93.

[35] *Ibid.*, pp. 154–62. [36] *Spirit and Reality*, p. 168.

[37] The title of a remarkable book on the anti-apartheid struggle in South Africa by Helen Joseph. It is not irrelevant that this has been for her the way back into the life of the Spirit. In this she is, I suspect, representative of many in our age.

rate, for many, picketing and praying have become so assimilated that it is difficult to draw a line between them.

This has begun to show itself in what I believe is a new and significant form of contemporary spirituality. I tried to delineate it in an article I wrote for *New Christian*,[38] and I have adapted some material from it in the paragraphs that follow.

The essence of this spirituality is that it starts from life rather than works toward it. In distinction from the traditions I have previously mentioned, it seems so far to have flowered most in French-speaking Catholicism and American-speaking Protestantism. From the former, the classic is Michel Quoist's *Prayers of Life*. It begins from life just as it comes—the telephone, a five-pound note, the pornographic magazine, hunger, housing, a bald head—and turns it all not only into prayer but often poetry as well. "The Sea" is not only pure poetry but an example, by contrast rare in this genre, of equal sensitivity to nature and to that which "wears man's smudge and shares man's smell."[39]

Of the second, American, variety one may take Malcolm Boyd's collection *Are You Running with Me, Jesus?* This is Quoist in prose, prayer in the raw, with the last varnish gone. "All human life is there," as *The News of the World* advertisement claims, in all its warmth and all its lovelessness, laid bare before God. Malcolm Boyd, himself formerly in advertising, is an Episcopalian priest whose ministry has lain in state universities and civil rights. Section headings indicate the scope of this very worldly holiness: "Prayers for the Free Self," "Prayers for the Free Society," "Prayers in the City,"

[38] September 8, 1966; reprinted in *But That I Can't Believe!*, chap. 23.
[39] Gerard Manley Hopkins, "God's Grandeur."

"Meditations on Films," "Prayers for Sexual Freedom," and so on. What he calls in his introduction "the heretical gap" between the holy and the profane has quite disappeared. And he has followed this with a set of "secular meditations" called *Free to Live, Free to Die,* which is in many ways the best example yet of this prophetic spirituality.[40]

It was another Episcopalian priest, Robert Castle, who wrote the *Litany for the Ghetto* already referred to. Here there is such an identification between God and the city that grammar is strained to breaking-point in bringing together the *Thou* addressed and the third person indicative of those who *are* the city:

> O God, who lives in tenements, who goes to segregated schools, who is beaten in precincts, who is unemployed ...
>
> Help us to know you
>
> O God, who is cold in the slums of winter, whose playmates are rats—four-legged ones who live with you and two-legged ones who imprison you ...
>
> Help us to touch you

—and so on, ever nearer the bone.

If one were to try to sum up the marks of this mode, or mood, of prayer, certain things recur. Its controlling rubric

---

[40] See also Robert A. Raines, *Creative Brooding*, a collection of daily readings, each starting with an excerpt from a contemporary writer or journalist and leading through Biblical passages into prayer. Its method is to use the secular to "sharpen thought and provoke reflection." Alan Watts also speaks of "contemplation in its secular form" (*Behold the Spirit*, p. 233), which has always been one of the strengths of Zen.

might be the words of Coventry Patmore, "You may see the disc of Divinity quite clearly through the smoked glass of humanity, but not otherwise."[41] Indeed, its key preposition is "through." God is to be met in, with, and under, not apart from, response to the world and the neighbor. Its point of entry into God, the *ens realissimum,* is whatever *is* most real for the person concerned, however irreligious. Its form of the divine is more often than not the Son of Man incognito, whose presence is to be known obliquely, parabolically, brokenly—but always presently. Its style is that of a *secular mysticism,*[42] with each of these words equally stressed. There is—in Christ—no gulf, no difference even, between ordinary life and prayer. And, needless to say, any special holy language or devotional diction is out. The "thees" and the "thous" have gone without trace.

And yet it is saturated with awareness of the world as *Thou* —and with the meeting through it of "the eternal *Thou.*" As an art form it is liberally interspersed with vocatives— usually "Lord," in Boyd as often as not "Jesus." The Deity is invoked freely, even chummily. It reads like devotional Don Camillo, with "the Lord" always around, as a gnome on the shoulder or a friend at the side.

And this conversational tone is odd, because Malcolm Boyd says specifically that he has come to see prayer as "not so much talking to God" as "just sharing his presence." It appears indeed often more like Jesus sharing Boyd's presence and being conveniently at hand to compare notes with. But

---

[41] *The Rod, the Root, and the Flower* (London, 1895), p. 45.

[42] W. R. Comstock uses the same phrase, instancing as examples, among others, Ludwig Wittgenstein and Simone Weil ("Theology after the 'Death of God,'" *Cross Currents,* 56 [1966], 294–98).

even at its best, as in Quoist, there is the sense of talking to a third Person, apart from and invisible to the person whose concern engages one. Does this take the *Thou* of the other with real seriousness and do justice to the fact that the claim of the unconditional must be met *in him* and *through him* —even if it is not possible or natural to say "Lord, Lord"?

The inauthenticity of this somewhat embarrassing talk contrasts at times jarringly with the ruthless honesty and economy of the general "style." I suspect it is the residual influence of the supranaturalist projection that still requires this third Person if the exercise is to qualify as "prayer."[43] Is there a relic here of what I called the "telstar" image, of re-directing messages off a celestial Being? Has this been replaced—instead of demythologized—by a three-cornered conversation? The current "pop" prayer idiom, with its stage asides, strikes me in fact as less truly incarnational than the (far more reserved) Quaker tradition of spirituality, which has its ambience much more *in* the Spirit and sees the Presence rather in terms of that which lights up every man from *within,* or, as Buber would put it, is "*between* man and man."

The strength of this contemporary prayer-style is that it is inescapably personal. It knows God as given in response to the whole of life as *Thou.* Its weakness is that it is often artificially personalistic—envisaging God as a separate *Thou.* Is "O Lord" the last remnant of the poetic diction of a bygone age—or is it unavoidable? And if the latter, can we use rather than stumble at the "myth"?

[43] Toward the end of *Are You Running with Me, Jesus?* (e.g. in the "Meditations on Films" and the "Prayers for Sexual Freedom") it is noticeable that the interjections "Jesus" and "Lord" become increasingly incidental. In *Free to Live, Free to Die* they have disappeared entirely, without the meditations ceasing to be prayers except in the purely formal sense.

The *Litany for the Ghetto* with its identification of God with the scene rather than the spectator here seems to me to have the advantage. It has provoked the inevitable charge of pantheism. But it is not asserting a metaphysical identity between God and the city; it is simply affirming that at the given moment for the subject in prayer this is where, and who, God is—and there is no turning aside, not even to Another.

In spirituality as in theology I find myself returning to the utterly personal panentheism of the God dwelling incognito at the heart of all things. Indeed, there is ultimately no line between a living theology and "a whole spirituality." So much is this the case that I will repeat in closing, to sum up what I have said on prayer, words that I originally wrote of the vocation held out to the theologian:

It is a call in the first place not to relevance in any slick sense but to exposure, to compassion, sensitivity, awareness and integrity. It is the call to bear reality, more reality than it is easy or indeed possible for a human being to bear unaided. It is to be with God in his world. And in each epoch or culture the place of the theologian is to stand as near as he may to the "creative center" of God's world in his day.[44]

That is also the place of the man of prayer. It is indeed "the longest journey" upon which a human being can embark.

The function of the map, whether in doctrinal or in ascetical theology, is, by the projection it uses, to assist rather than hinder that journey inwards. So, finally, let us return to the map, to see whether there is anything more adequate we can draw in order to represent the center and goal of the whole quest.

[44] *The New Reformation?*, p. 75.

CHAPTER SEVEN

Beyond the God of Theism

The God above or beyond God: such is the concept on which Tillich ends his psychological study *The Courage to Be*.[1] It is heady language, dangerous language. It is language from which one instinctively draws back. I sheered off it and deliberately refused to use it, among so much else from Tillich, in *Honest to God*. For it has a long theological history, strewn with many warnings. Those who have spoken about going above the God of theism have usually sunk below it; and those who have aimed at a suprapersonal Deity have ended more often than not with one that is less than fully personal. From Apostolic times onwards, Gnostics, Marcionites, Theosophists have sought to pass beyond the creator-God of Biblical faith only to lose themselves in airy speculation.

Yet, as constantly, the profoundest and greatest minds return to the theme. Above all has this been true of the mystics, and among them many of the giants—Eckhart, Boehme, Angelus Silesius, Ruysbroeck. Eckhart's distinction between *Gott* and *Gottheit,* the God of revelation and the ineffable mystery of the Godhead, like Boehme's *Ungrund* or abyss of Being, has been drawn upon by modern writers like Berdyaev

[1] (Welwyn, Eng., 1952), pp. 172–78.

and Tillich, who are certainly not unaware of the perils of such talk. One cannot simply dismiss a quest by such men. One is bound to ask what impels them to it.

Fundamentally, what impels them is an acute awareness of the limitations of any theology that describes God, the final reality behind and beyond all existence, in terms of *a* Person or indeed *a* God. That it has done this has been the strength as well as the weakness of popular theism (professional theology has always been more careful—and more remote). For it has presented God to men as a God they can visualize, a Being not too unlike themselves, who does things, who enters into real relationships with them, who can be prayed to and blamed. And the power of such a presentation is that it has done justice to the reality of encounter, of relationship, of over-againstness at the heart of the spiritual awareness. Personality implies a genuine frontier between *I* and *Thou* which preserves the freedom both of man and of God. Destroy this delimitation and both God and man are swallowed up in a boundless impersonal Absolute, in "the dark silence in which all lovers lose themselves" (Ruysbroeck).

Yet the price of this presentation is to depict God as a Being among beings, as a Person contrasted with the rest of reality, "as a self which has a world, as an ego which is related to a thou, as a cause which is separated from its effect."[2] Philosophically and spiritually this representation of the Divine has been under constant criticism from acute minds and sensitive souls who cannot be ignored. Such a God has been found inadequate to carry the spiritual quest. And this is becoming more, not less, evident as new dimensions in physics,

[2] *Ibid.*, p. 175.

in evolution, in psychology, in spirituality are constantly being opened up. The contemporary case for something that breaks through the limitations of traditional Western personalism is well made in F. C. Happold's *Religious Faith and Twentieth-Century Man*. Leslie Dewart also appeals to a widespread popular sense of the insufficiency of traditional categories:

The typical experience of the disaffiliated religious person today is that "God could not possibly be a person. He must be some kind of cosmic force." This is surely a naive view to the degree that it implies that God is less than man. But this is not all that this common expression connotes. It also means that God is, rather than a center of being to which we are drawn, an expansive force which impels persons to go out from and beyond themselves. This expression represents an effort, born of understandable impatience, to transcend the primitive God-being, God-object and God-person of absolute theism. The truth that that crude expression so mistakenly conceives may yet be redeemed in the future by Christian theism.[3]

Unfortunately this is his last word on the personality of God. His book is more helpful for the fascinating trails it suggests than for its follow-through. And this merely reflects the fact that it is much easier to sense the constrictions than to pass constructively beyond them.

Yet before attempting this I am concerned to try to avoid the gaping pitfall of doing less than justice to the reality to be represented in the illusion of doing more. "Absolute theism" or "Western personalism" may have its limitations, but at least it has affirmed, in Feuerbach's words, that "to predicate personality of God is... to declare personality as the

[3] *The Future of Belief*, p. 189.

absolute essence."[4] In questioning the *way* it does this, it is very easy to question—and even more to appear to question —the central affirmation it is concerned to safeguard. Indeed, in trying to move out or on from even the most traditionally personalistic ways of speaking of God one is so constantly accused, both by churchmen and by humanists, of "no longer believing in a personal God" that, at the risk of some repetition, it may be desirable to preface any further exploration by going over again the ground that must not be surrendered.

In one sense, it is perfectly true that one *is* questioning belief in a personal God, if by that is meant that commitment to the personal as the central interpretative category of the whole of reality involves being tied to the particular image or projection that represents this as *a* divine Person. But to question the image is of much less significance than to abandon the reality. And therefore, though technically it may be correct to say that one "no longer believes in a personal God," it is far more false than true. What one is concerned to affirm is the conviction theism has always been concerned to make central. And, as we have sought to show, this conviction is given *in the first instance* not as belief in the existence of a Being but as apprehension of a relational reality.

Perhaps one can try to explicate this further by risking an analogy—though every analogy involves the danger of being as misleading as it is helpful. But at least this is a well-tried and Biblical analogy, as well as a personal one—that of mother-love. "Can a woman forget her sucking child, that she should have no compassion on the son of her womb?" asks Isaiah in the name of God. Yes, "even these may forget,

[4] *The Essence of Christianity* (New York, 1957), p. 99.

yet I will not forget you."[5] The primal experience of being human is to find oneself held in a relationship of sustaining, claiming love. This is the given, gracious context of all human life, and it is through this relationship of more than biological stimulus and response that the infant is gradually drawn out to distinctively personal existence and responsibility. The law of all life, that "through thee I am," is given additional significance in the case of human beings. For it is only through the grace and claim of the *Thou* that the individual comes to know himself as *I*. The umbilical cord of responsibility supersedes the purely physical connection between mother and child. This relationship is invisible, though it is mediated by the visible features, especially of the face. And it gradually broadens, or should broaden, into a fully adult, free relationship with society and the world at large, without however ever losing its fundamental structure of grace and claim, response and responsibility.

It is some such relatedness which the Judaeo-Christian tradition sees as supplying the context and structure of all life. Everything is held in being and given its distinctive character by the fact that it is essentially and inescapably response to a creative, evocative "word" of grace and claim, drawing it out and upwards to a love in which alone it can find its fulfillment and freedom. In man this response becomes conscious as responsibility.[6] The divine grace and claim is invisible, intangible—and indeed undefinable in and for itself —and yet is mediated through whatever "face" of God presents itself. It comes, in all its reassuring givenness and in all

---

[5] Isaiah 49.15.

[6] This theme receives classic statement in Brunner's great book *Man in Revolt*.

its disturbing power, through the whole of existence, impersonal and personal. But the *quality* of its graciousness and claim are sensed as *more like* those of a personal relationship than of an impersonal, of a free, spiritual communion which it is possible to reject than of a purely physical connection which can only be accepted.

Hence the picture of a Person behind the phenomena, a supreme Father-figure corresponding to the earthly mother-figure. Yet this is anthropomorphism, creating God in our own image. There is nothing wrong with it, as long as we recognize it for what it is. And the best way to recognize it is to switch to another metaphor, where anyone can see the difference.

"The Lord is my rock and my fortress," sings the Psalmist,[7] in language used by many Biblical writers. The "rock" is a symbol for the security which is also an essential element in mother-love. God is the foundation of life, the ground of being, the undergirding reality that prevents everything falling through into meaninglessness and dread. To affirm that "the Lord is my rock" is to affirm that there is a bottom, an utterly reliable and unshakable basis to living. It is the same trust that is expressed in more human terms by saying that "underneath are the everlasting arms."[8] Yet no one supposes that this means that there is in any sense a Rock, somewhere around, like a cosmic Rock of Gibraltar, which must "exist" if the whole experience is not to be an illusion.

"Father" is a much ampler and more adequate metaphor for this security. The security of a rock is impersonal, hard, unfeeling. It could not serve the Psalmist who wanted to

[7] Psalm 18.2.
[8] Deuteronomy 33.27.

147

affirm that "like as a father pitieth his own children, even so is the Lord merciful unto them that fear him."[9] Yet the metaphor of "father" by very reason of its greater adequacy contains the greater danger that its metaphorical character will be forgotten. Men can easily say that God *is* a father in a way that they can never seriously say that he *is* a rock. And they can go on to say that the reality to which the metaphor points can be true only if there *is* a Being who *does* exist, with these attributes, somewhere around. "Otherwise," they will ask, "what do you mean by talking about love as the ultimate reality, unless there is a Lover? What do you mean by talking of God in personal terms unless there is a Person? If that is what you believe in, then we can understand it (even if we cannot believe it). But if you do not accept that there is such a Person, then it is merely confusing and dishonest to go on speaking of 'God.' For the word must refer to this Being— or mean nothing."

So the familiar argument runs. But in fact the New Testament says that "God is love" (not that it means this literally or univocally, any more than when it says "God is light" or "God is spirit"): the proposition "God is a Being who loves" is a transposition (as is the familiar mistranslation "God is *a* Spirit"). The conviction that reality is reliable, not merely in a rock-like way, but in the kind of way in which a person can be trusted, is transposed into belief in an ultimate divine Person. It is a harmless and indeed a profoundly helpful symbol. The Bible, and the New Testament in particular, is full of language speaking of God in terms such as "Father!," "my Father," "like a father"—though it is noteworthy that it never says directly that God is a father, any more than it

9 Psalm 103.13.

148

says that he is a rock. "My rock," "our rock" indicate the typically existential, rather than metaphysical, character of such affirmations. And the same applies to "father." But to talk of God *as though* he *were* an invisible father seated in heaven presented no difficulty—let alone stumbling-block—when the whole universe was peopled with invisible personal beings in a quite naïve way. In an age in which mythology was taken entirely naturally as description of how things are there was no need to differentiate or to stress the "as if." Jesus could use it quite freely as a way of making vivid the utterly personal relationship of trust and dependence in which his whole life was grounded. It caused no barrier to belief, and it made God immediately and obviously real—though the Bible is constantly warning against the danger of *all* images, and not merely of graven ones.

But now, as we have tried to indicate, the simplistic representation of God as a Person is the source or at any rate the occasion of great stumbling—as well as, still, of great comfort and faith. It produces in many sheer unbelief. Such beings, it is held, simply do not exist (or at least there is no evidence for them), and the reality of the God-relationship is quickly made to turn on quite extraneous arguments and proofs. In an age of science and technology the image of an invisible Superman personally creating phenomena as a potter makes a pot strikes more people as incredible than helpful. And in an age of planning a cosmic planner who cannot or does not prevent disasters merely appears supremely incompetent or grossly culpable.

On more and more occasions it is positively imperative to sit loose to the image—or even to discard it—if the truth it is intended to represent is to be maintained. And I am profound-

ly convinced that the truth does remain. For this reason I believe it is more important to insist on the continuity of belief
in God as personal—and to retain the word "God" however
loaded—than to give it up. The reality of being surrounded,
sustained, claimed abides—even though there is a healthy
process of detachment going on from certain childish notions
of dependence which religion has often fostered[10] (contrary
to everything in the New Testament's equation of "sonship"
with the maturity and freedom of man come of age).[11] And
the need to speak in some way of "God" represents the conviction that this encompassing reality, the element in which
man lives and moves and has his being, is not merely ma-
terialistic or even humanistic. The question is *how* one gives
expression to this conviction. Certainly it is not adequate to
describe the reality in impersonal categories—though it re-
veals itself in many impersonal "faces." Yet to envisage it as
embodied in a Person diminishes it and trivializes it. If the
only alternative to a personal God is a less than personal Absolute, then let us by all means retain the former. Yet it is impossible to escape the fact that this is a serious obstacle to faith
for modern secular man, as, indeed, it has always been for
Oriental religious man. There are only too many today who
do not think it possible to believe in God as personal *at all* unless it be in the old image. Can we get beyond this dilemma,

[10] Berdyaev writes: "Schleiermacher is wrong when he says that the religious feeling is a feeling of dependence. Dependence is an earthly thing.
We might have better reason for saying it is a feeling of independence. We
may speak of God only by analogy with what is revealed in the depths of
spiritual experience" (*Truth and Revelation,* translated in Donald A. Low-
rie's Berdyaev anthology *Christian Existentialism* [London, 1965], p. 45).
I should prefer to substitute the word "interdependence."
[11] See especially John 8.31–38 and Galatians 4.1–7.

this false either-or, of having to be atheists or theists in the old sense? This is the question to which we must now return.

I should like to focus it by seeing it through the mind—the often strange, contorted, visionary mind—of one man. He is the relatively little known Victorian English naturalist and mystic Richard Jefferies.[12] Part of his fascination is that he was almost totally self-educated, with many of the oddities of judgment and perspective which this tends to produce,[18] but with a vision both into nature and, as it were, through nature that makes him a spiritual brother of writers whom he had not read nor probably even heard of. The reason for his particular interest as a mystic is that he was an atheist, in the sense of rejecting—often with vehemence—the only theism he knew, with, nevertheless, an intense sense of and insatiable openness to what he called "the Beyond."

At first sight he appears to be a typical nature-mystic with an overwhelming sense of the immanence of the spiritual in the natural:

Through every grass blade in the thousand, thousand grasses; through the million leaves, veined and edge-cut, on bush and tree; through the song-notes and the marked feathers of the birds; through the insects' hum and the color of the butterflies; through

---

[12] His most remarkable—and here most relevant—book is his spiritual autobiography, *The Story of My Heart,* of which it may be said, as Walt Whitman wrote of one of his own: "This is no book / Who touches this, touches a man." Of the many books on Jefferies see, for a contemporary verdict, W. Besant, *The Eulogy of Richard Jefferies*; for a modern biography using the evidence of unpublished notebooks, S. J. Looker and Crichton Porteous, *Richard Jefferies: Man of the Fields*; and for a literary criticism, W. J. Keith, *Richard Jefferies: A Critical Study.*

[13] E.g., his rejection of any notion of evolution and his naïve theory of the eventual capacity of man physically to live forever.

the soft warm air, the flecks of clouds dissolving—I used them all for prayer.[14]

He has an exquisite, almost excruciating, sense of the presence of the Beyond pressing upon him through earth, sky, and sea, and above all through the rays of the sun. Yet he has no sentimental illusions about nature. There is, he recognizes, "nothing human in nature," nothing, that is, that cares a jot for personal values. Indeed, it is anti-human. Nor is there any god in nature, no evidence of design or benevolent purpose. Like the Preacher of Ecclesiastes, he is forced to the conclusion that "time and chance happen to . . . all."[15] In this sense he is as skeptical as any nineteenth-century atheist.

And yet he is not, cannot be, content to leave things there. Indeed, his atheism is not negative or destructive. Rather, the idea of a God is, for him, totally inadequate for the reality which the soul touches but cannot hope to grasp. He sees it as "an invisible idol." "The mind goes on and requires more . . . something higher than a god,"[16] "something infinitely higher than deity."[17] And he links this with the need to press beyond the "three ideas" concerning the inner consciousness of man which have in the course of civilization so far been "wrested from the unknown"—"the existence of the soul, immortality, the deity."[18] The fashioning of these three ideas corresponds, we may say, to the stage in the description of reality that Van Peursen designates as the ontological.[19] The soul, immortality, and God are conceived in terms of sub-

[14] *The Story of My Heart* (Swan Library edition; London, 1933), p. 15.
[15] Ecclesiastes 9.11. [16] *The Story of My Heart*, p. 198.
[17] *Ibid.*, p. 206. [18] *Ibid.*, pp. 52–61 *passim.*
[19] See p. 34 above.

stantial existence, and men's intimations of the Beyond are given "objective," metaphysical reality in these imaginable entities. And Jefferies has no desire to go back on them: they are indeed pointers, "stepping-stones" to a "fourth idea" or, rather, to an illimitable series of ideas, "an immense ocean over which the mind can sail, upon which the vessel of thought has not yet been launched." "The mind of so many thousand years has worked round and round inside the circle of these three ideas as a boat on an island lake. Let us haul it over the belt of land, launch on the ocean, and sail onwards."

Meanwhile for Jefferies the God of theism must be transcended as far too small. It is this God that for him must die, and not simply the God of deism, of absolute transcendence, whom it seems Altizer is railing at. The God of theism is a legitimate protest against monism, in the name of a genuine relationship, a real duality of *I* and *Thou,* such as personality requires. And yet it is not able to transcend dualism. It polarizes God and the world *as though* they existed alongside each other in unresolved juxtaposition. This dualism runs through all the characteristic language of Western theism. It speaks of

> God *and* the world
> Heaven *and* earth
> Eternity *and* time
> The infinite *and* the finite
> Transcendence *and* immanence
> The one *and* the many
> Good *and* evil
> The divine nature *and* the human in Christ.

And so one could go on. Like Descartes' principles of thought and extension, neither can be reduced to the other. Yet neither has the power to unify the other with itself. God is on *one side* of each pair of opposites.

But there is a powerful and perennial tradition—in philosophy, in mysticism, in Oriental religion—which refuses to remain content with this situation, and constantly yearns to break through to a non-duality, to a *coincidence* of opposites, to a higher all-embracing unity. "By the Beyond," wrote Richard Jefferies in the notebooks of his last pain-wracked years, "I mean the Idea of the *whole:* that would fill the sky." It is the same vision as that of the thirteenth-century Umbrian mystic, Angela of Foligno:

The eyes of my soul were opened, and I beheld the plenitude of God, wherein I did comprehend the whole world, both here and beyond the sea, the abyss and the ocean and all things. In all these things I beheld naught save the divine power, in a manner assuredly indescribable; so that through excess of marvelling the soul cried with a loud voice, saying: "The whole world is full of God."[20]

There is the characteristic paradox that the whole world is *in* God and, at the same time, that the whole world is full *of* God. As Meister Eckhart puts it, "The more God is in all things, the more he is outside them. The more he is within, the more he is without."[21]

The overcoming of the duality which divides even Creator and creature is, of course, a commonplace not only in Hinduism but in the Christian mystics. The so-called "mystic copula," which says with the Hindu *tat tvam asi*—"Thou (the

---

[20] From her *Liber Visionum,* quoted by F. C. Happold, *Religious Faith and Twentieth Century Man* (Harmondsworth, Eng., 1966), p. 131. H. de Lubac notes the influence of this mystic on Teilhard de Chardin in *The Religion of Teilhard de Chardin,* p. 26.

[21] Quoted by Happold, *Religious Faith . . . ,* p. 130.

self) art That (God)"—or with Angelus Silesius, "He who seeks God must become God,"[22] is not asserting, as was said earlier,[23] a metaphysical equation, so that all the attributes of God are transferred to the finite self. It is affirming an identification which passes beyond what Nicholas of Cusa called "the door of the coincidence of opposites." And God for Nicholas is to be seen always "beyond the coincidence of contradictories . . . , and nowhere this side thereof."[24] In other words, God is not *one* of the poles of traditional theism, but transcends these inevitable finite distinctions. To express this within the logic of non-contradiction is of course finally impossible. But the same writer struggles with an answer when in this philosophical meditation he asks of God, "How then dost thou create things other than thyself—for thou wouldst seem to create thyself?" and goes on:

Yet this is no real difficulty, since with thee creation and existence are the same. And creating and being created alike are naught else than the sharing of thy Being among all, that thou mayest be All in all, and yet mayest abide freed from all. For to call into being things which are not is to make Nothing a sharer in Being: thus to call is to create, while to share is to be created. And beyond this coincidence of creating and being created art thou, Absolute and Infinite God, neither creating nor creatable, albeit all things are what they are because thou art.[25]

This may appear abstruse and rarified mystification—or, on the other hand, a commonplace of what many of the great-

---

[22] Quoted by Berdyaev, *Spirit and Reality*, p. 143, who also cites from the same source these other equally horrifying sayings: "I am as great as God, he is as little as I"; "When I with God into God am transformed"; "It is I must be the sun, to give color with my beams to the colorless sea of the Godhead entire."

[23] See p. 87 above.   [24] *The Vision of God,* chap. 9.

[25] *Ibid.,* chap. 12.

est minds and spirits have always been seeking to say. There is nothing new about it. What is new, I believe, is that in our generation its relevance is no longer confined to upper reaches of ascetic and philosophical theology. For a revolution is taking place which is exposing the inadequacies of the theistic image of God, which has hitherto served for ordinary "lay" thought and spirituality. Windows have been thrown open on a vastly larger world. There has been extensive—and intensive—popularization of insights into aspects of reality which threaten to break the thought-barriers of traditional Western theism. There has been a communications-explosion in psychology, in mysticism, in parapsychology, in the effects of psychedelic drugs, in a living awareness of Hindu, Buddhist, and Sufi spirituality, and so on and so on. One has only to mention the wide influence of deeply serious writers like Jung and Tillich, Aldous and Julian Huxley, Arnold Toynbee and Thomas Merton. This means that what were before marginal speculations have become frontier problems. The issues of this chapter—of how one thinks beyond the God of theism—are raised, for instance, quite explicitly and urgently in such books of popular "lay" theology as F. C. Happold's *Religious Faith and Twentieth Century Man,* Alan Watts' playful, perverse, or profound book (according to how one looks at it) *Beyond Theology: The Art of Godmanship,* and the Chicago journalist William Braden's study, *The Private Sea: An Inquiry into the Religious Implications of LSD.*

Moreover, in all this the effect must not be underrated of the revolutions that have taken place in the myths, models, and thought-patterns used to describe the purely physical world. Both matter and spirit present themselves very differently than they did even a generation ago. They are thought of as far less divergent and as far less "substantial." And I would basically agree with Happold when he predicts that

The religious thought-forms of twentieth-century man will represent a new fusion of religious and scientific "myths," mystically (in the sense we are using the term) interpreted, accompanied, particularly among the more sensitive types, by a growth in spirituality, and by a deeper sanctification of secular life, as the sacred and the profane are more and more seen as one.[26]

Watts points out that the modern scientific way of *describing* the identity of things and events is much nearer the way in which the mystic *feels* them.[27] Causes and effects are no longer viewed as separate occurrences, bumping into each other like billiard balls, but as aspects of a single event. What anything *is* is seen to depend more and more on its relation to the "system" of which it is a part. The behavior of things and objects is viewed as the behavior of "fields"—spatial, gravitational, magnetic, or social. As he says, "these unitary, relational, and 'fieldish' ways of thinking give immense plausibility to non-dualist or pantheist (to be frightfully exact 'pan-*en*theist') types of metaphysic."[28] And he makes the good point that the defect of what he calls "theological monarchism," or a Supreme Being type of theology, is not that it is anthropomorphic but that it is (now) bad anthropomorphism:

To construct a God in the human image is objectionable only to the extent that we have a poor image of ourselves, for example, as egos in bags of skin. But as we can begin to visualize man as

[26] *Religious Faith and Twentieth-Century Man*, p. 122.
[27] *Beyond Theology*, pp. 226–27.   [28] *Ibid.*, p. 225.

the behavior of a unified field—immensely complex and comprising the whole universe—there is less and less reason against conceiving God in *that* image. To go deeper and deeper into oneself is also to go farther and farther out into the universe, until, as the physicist well knows, we reach the domain where three-dimensional, sensory images are no longer valid.[29]

This convergence of the models appropriate to the scientific and the theological exploration is relevant also as an answer to one of the major traditional hazards of trying to push "beyond" the God of theism. Historically this seems always to have been associated with a movement to get further and further *away* from the natural order. In Gnosticism, the God "above" the Demiurge who created this world was to be found by passing through and out the other side of all the spheres of material existence. In Neo-platonism, which so powerfully influenced Christian mysticism by way of Pseudo-Dionysius, the One was to be gained at the expense of the many, by the flight of the alone to the Alone. In Hinduism and in many forms of Buddhism (though others are more incarnational), salvation is to be attained by negation of the world of *maya* and *samsara*. But today any relevant theology, like any relevant spirituality, must come through what Berdyaev calls the "realization" (that is, the fuller incarnation or materialization) of spirit.

This applies to each of the "three ideas" which Jefferies saw as needing to be transcended. "The soul" can no longer be thought of (as in the period of ontology) as an individual, nonmaterial, substance implanted in the body to which it in no real sense belongs. Rather, if we are to go on using the word, it must be related to the whole form of the personal in

[29] *Ibid.*, p. 222.

its spiritual aspect. Similarly, "immortality" cannot be seen (as Jefferies recognized) in terms of something in man which is not dissolved by physical death and which "goes on." Rather, it is a dimension to the whole of life as personal, represented more adequately by the New Testament phrase "eternal life." It is better described as "the life beyond myself" than merely "life beyond death," and it is given cosmic expression in the Jewish-Christian myth of the "resurrection" of the whole body of history.[30] In the same way, "God" is not to be understood as an Ego over against the world, *a* Spirit in contrast with created matter. Rather, if again we are to go on using the term, it must relate to that which compels us to speak of the whole of reality in terms of personal spirit, the transcendent source and goal of all being—in all things and through all things and above all things.

Ultimately in speaking of God all words are bound to fail. Yet rather than end in final aposiopesis, there is perhaps one more thing that can be said. One of the insights of our century is that the trans-personal character of God is better expressed not by envisaging him as a bigger and better Individual, nor as a sort of Hobbesian collective Personality incorporating all other persons, but in terms of the interpersonal. This is the result of applying "field" or relational thinking to persons as well as to things. For Buber has taught us that in the beginning—and in the end—is not the individual, the *I* or the *Thou,* but the nexus *I-Thou.* And the whole of reality too must ultimately be seen in terms, not of a God, a monarchical Being supreme among individual entities, but of a divine "field" in which the finite *Thous* are constituted what they

[30] See *In the End, God* (2d ed.), chaps. 8 and 9.

are in the freedom of a wholly personalizing love. In the same vein, Berdyaev, summing up what he calls "the pivotal idea" of his *Spirit and Reality,* says that the only justification of anthropomorphism is that "God is like a *whole humanity* rather than like nature, society, or concept."[31] The pledge of ultimate Reality within this world, the sign of the Kingdom, is what Dumitriu describes as "that dense and secret undergrowth which is wholly composed of personal events." But it is Teilhard de Chardin who has taken this idea to its most daring limits in the vision which closes *The Phenomenon of Man.* He sees the universe as pointing to "the hyperpersonal, beyond the collective," in which God is "the Center of centers" in an interlocking web of free spiritual relationship in which the All and the Personal are no longer exclusive.

This is the vision, too, to which the New Testament points, of God as "all in all."[32] This passage is the charter of Christian panentheism. Yet it is, as its context in I Corinthians 15 makes abundantly clear, an eschatological panentheism. This does not mean, for the New Testament, that it is something that will only be true *after* everything else.[33] It is the truth "in Christ" now. As the Epistle to the Hebrews puts it, "We do not yet see everything in subjection" to man—that is, to personal purpose. "But we see Jesus ... crowned with glory and honor."[34] And it is this, symbolically, that the Christian sees as the first fruits and guarantee of the whole cosmic process. The God who was *in* Christ is the God who is and must be

[31] P. 187. Italics mine.
[32] I Corinthians 15.28.
[33] For this I must again refer to my *In the End, God.*
[34] Hebrews 2.8–9.

in all. The model of panentheism is essentially an incarnational one. That is why I believe it is fundamentally appropriate to Christianity—in a way that deism or pantheism or even theism is not—without being exclusively Christian. And, *per contra,* I also believe that the most appropriate model—perhaps the only appropriate model today—for a satisfactory theology of the Incarnation is a panentheistic one.

But that is another book.

Index